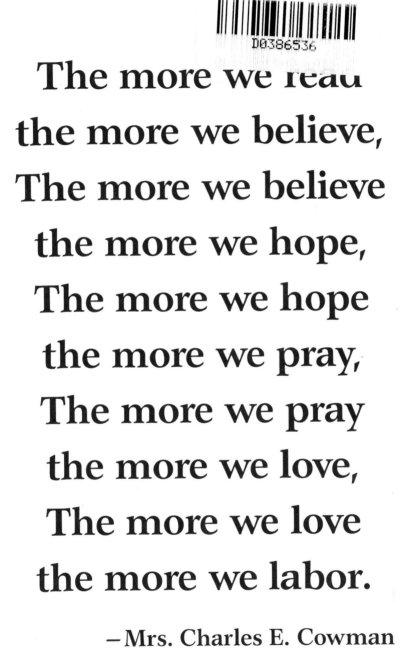

The more we read
the more we believe,
The more we believe
the more we hope,
The more we hope
the more we pray,
The more we pray
the more we love,
The more we love
the more we labor.

–Mrs. Charles E. Cowman

The People
You Meet
&
The Books
You Read

Other Books by Charles E. Jones

Life Is Tremendous
Motivational Classics
The Books You Read – Business Edition
The Books You Read – Professional Edition

You are the same today
as you will be five years from now
except for two things –

The
People You Meet and
THE BOOKS
You Read

edited by
Charles E. Jones

Foreword by
D. James Kennedy

Published by
Executive Books
P.O. Box 1044, Harrisburg PA 17108

Foreword

by D. James Kennedy, Ph.D.

The preacher must inevitably be a man of the Book and also a man of books. A good portion of his life must be committed to his library. A commitment to the ministry is likewise a commitment to the study. Here the pastor's mind and heart come into contact with the greatest thoughts and deepest feelings of the world's leading thinkers. The minister of the Word of God must, in addition to his study of the Bible, delve deeply into many related areas, such as: history, biography, science, literature, poetry, etc. All fields of knowledge must be made tributary to the great task of preaching. Great preachers have almost inevitably been men who were broadly read in the great books of the world. If this book serves to stimulate a greater interest in reading on the part of Christians, it will no doubt serve a very knowledgeable and useful purpose in the Kingdom of God.

Og Mandino CPAE

Many years ago, when I was just about as complete a failure as one can become, I began to spend a good deal of time in libraries, looking for some answers. Where had I gone wrong? How could I possibly have fouled up my life so badly? And, was it too late for me . . . a thirty-five year old wanderer with only a high school education?

I found all the answers I needed in that golden vein of ore that every library has. The advice from the books helped to change my life. I read with an open mind and a burning desire to change. . . .

This marvelous book that you are now holding is unique . . . a shopping list, ready, to guide you to the very best work that man and woman has written dealing with many areas of life. Search these pages carefully and I am certain that you will discover exactly the book or books that will help you to deal with your specific problem, whatever it may be. Just think of the time alone that this precious reference will save you in your personal search for the answers you need in order to reach your full potential.

We all need help. There is no such thing as a self-made man or woman. Charles "Tremendous" Jones has performed a miracle through this book. He has created a vehicle, a channel if you will, that will lead you to the perfect specialist that can cure whatever is preventing you from making the progress you deserve. You are a miracle, God's greatest miracle, and now you have a guide that will lead you to the answers you need and prove to yourself, as well as others, how great you really are. Happy hunting, good reading, and joyful living!

Contents

Sections
The Love and Power of God Through Books 17
A Book I'd Like to Share 31
The Book 173
A Book I'd Like to Share 193
Great Thoughts on Reading 261

The Love and Power of God Through Books

Ken Taylor and a Book 18
William Borden and a Book 22
The Blessed Library: Bishop Joseph Hall 23
Charles Colson and a Book 24
Bert Decker and a Book 26
John Newton and Thomas à Kempis 27
David Livingstone: The Right Book at the Right Time 28
Jonathan Edwards and Books 29
David Brainerd and Jonathan Edwards 30

A Book I'd Like to Share 31

Recommender: *Book Title:*

College Presidents

Lee, Mark   A Catalogue of Sins 32
Lease, Stuart   Spiritual Leadership 32
Walword, John   He that Is Spiritual 33
Hostetter, D. Ray   Imitation of Christ 33
Aldrich, Joe   Mystery of Marriage 33
Armerding, Hudson   Through the Valley of the Kwai 34
Cook, Robert A.   The Law of Faith 35
Guillermin, Pierre   Strategy for Living 36
Hungerpiller, W. D.   The Battle for the Bible 37
McRae, William   The Knowledge of the Holy 38
Sweeting, George   Bush Aglow 39
Williams, Bill   Your God Is Too Small 40
Kesler, Jay   The Presence of the Kingdom 41
Jenson, Ronald   Authentic Christianity 42
MacArthur, John Jr.   The Treasury of Scripture Knowledge 43

Adams, Buford   The Problem of Pain 44
Austin, William   Evangelism & the Sovereignty of God 45
Baker, A. A.   The Life of Missionary C.T. Studd 46
Batten, Joe   The Sermon on the Mount 47
Baxter, J. Sidlow   Strong's Exhaustive Concordance 48
Bayly, Joseph   The Works of the Mind 49

Beebe, Wally   Hudson Taylor's Spiritual Secret 50
Bellig, Jacob   Extraordinary Living – Ordinary Man 51
Bergen, Peter   Communications: Key to Marriage 52
Berman, Bernie   The Compassionate Touch 53
Betzer, Dan   The Knowledge of the Holy 54
Bickel, Bruce   Distinguishing Traits of
         Christian Character 55
Bittenbender, Melvin   How I Learned to Meditate 56

Professional Football   57–59

Blackledge, Todd   Proverbs
Shearin, Joe   Study of Romans
McLeod, Mike   Answers to Tough Questions
Andrews, William   Ten Dates for Mates
Hancock, Anthony   Garden of Eden
McPherson, Debbie   The Mike MacIntosh Story
Woudenberg, Jamie   For Better or for Best
Birdsong, Carl   Strengthening Your Grip 60
Bland, Glenn   As a Man Thinketh 61
Boone, Pat   The Cross and the Switchblade 62

William Borden and Books   63

Brandt, Henry   Abundant Living 64
Bright, William   God's Best Secrets 65
Briscoe, D. Stuart   Romans 66
Brown, W. Steven   The Richest Man in Babylon 67
Brown, Preacher   Romans 68

Educators – Bible Teachers   69–74

Burks, David   The Aroma of Christ
Marty, Martin   Large Catechism of Martin Luther
Cawood, John   Our Lord Prays for His Own
Smith, Wilbur   The Crises of the Christ
McGee, J. Vernon   Living Messages of the Books of the
Morris, Henry   Strong's Concordance
Rosenthal, Marvin   Grace
Whitcomb, John   That You Might Believe
Bittle, A. Richart   Here's How by Who's Who
Burnham, David   Knowing God 75

Great Missionaries and Books   76
William Carey and David Livingstone

Cho, Paul   Tough Times Never Last 77
Chow, Moses   Queen of the Dark Chamber 78
Christenson, Evelyn   With Christ in the School of Prayer 79
Coe, Douglas   St. Francis of Assisi 80

Coleman, Robert	Pensees 81
Cook, William	Spirit-Controlled Temperament 82
Coulter, Harold	The Life that Wins 83
Criswell, W.A.	Morning & Evening 84
Crouch, C. Van	Success, Motivation & the Scriptures 85
Crowley, Mary	The Mark of a Christian 86
Davey, James A.	The Weight of Glory 87
Davey, James E.	Twenty Centuries of Great Preaching 88
Davidson, Guy	Move Ahead with Possibility Thinking 89
Dixon, Carl	Failure: The Back Door to Success 90
Dobson, James	A History of English Speaking Peoples 91
Domenick, S. J.	Life Is Tremendous 92
Duff, Stephen	The Pursuit of God 93
Dunlap, H. Creighton	The Bishop of Wall Street 94
Dunn, Bruce	The Great Evangelical Disaster 95
DuPlessis, David	Pilgrim's Progress 96
Eaton, Ralph	Freedom of Simplicity 97
Edwards, Jon	Bruchko 98
Evans, Norm	If Only He Knew 99

Interdenominational Ministries 100–101

Engstrom, Ted	The Training of the Twelve
Eshelman, Ira	The Holy Spirit in Today's World
McCalister, Jack	The Shepherd Psalm
Sanchez, George	The Pursuit of God
Falwell, Jerry	The Normal Christian Life 102
Ferrier, Dale	The Lord of the Rings 103
Fitzpatrick, Herb	The Shadow of the Broad Brim 104
Galloway, Dale	The Fourth Dimension 105
Gannett, Alden	He that Is Spiritual 106
Glass, Bill	The One Minute Manager 107
Grant, Dave	The Taste for the Other 108
Griset, Lorin	The Lords of the Earth 109
Grounds, Vernon	Ethics of Freedom 110
Haggai, John	The Jesus Style 111
Haggai, Tom	If God Is in Charge 112

Chaplain United States Senate 113
Richard Halverson

Hartman, Jack	God's Smuggler 114
Heckman, Warren	Not Made for Defeat 115
Helle, Roger	Another Chance – How God Overrides Our Mistakes 116
Helton, Max	Quiet Talks on Power 117
Hendricks, Howard	The Seven Laws of Teaching 118

Hewett, Frank   Moving Heaven and Earth 119
Hill, Don   Still Higher for His Highest 120
Hillis, Dave   Understanding Christian Missions 121
Hobbs, Herschel   Preaching and Preachers 122
Hottel, Clarence   George Mueller, Man of Faith and Miracles 123
Hutson, Curtis   Deeper Experiences of Famous Christians 124

H. A. Ironside and Books 125

Janz, Jim   The Secret Kingdom 126
Johnson, Ken   Found: God's Will 127

Samuel Johnson and William Law 128

Johnston, Larry   Power Through Prayer 129
Jones, Gloria   That Incredible Christian 130
Jones, Jamie   I Dare You 131
Jones, Jeffrey   Perelandra 132
Jones, Jere   Oswald Chambers: An Unbribed Soul 133
Jones, Max   Holes in Time 134
Jones, Tracey   Hind's Feet on High Places 135

Adoniram Judson on Reading 136

Mrs. Adoniram Judson & Books 137

Kelly, Robert J.   Beyond Humiliation the Way of the Cross 138
Kennedy, D. James   Peace with God 139

Executives 140-141

Kraft, Daryl   Jeremiah
Frederick, Thomas   Christ at the Round Table
Kubiatowicz, Mike   How to Win Over Worry
Jent, Ben   Victorious Christian Living
Hitchcock, Harry   My Utmost for His Highest
Fisco, John M.   Spurgeons Devotional Bible
LaHaye, Tim   Temperament and the Christian Faith 142
Larson, Kenneth   The Making of a Man of God 143
Leonard, Jack   Life More Abundant 144
Lester, Tom   How Should We Then Live 145
Lewis, Bill   God's Workmanship 146
Lewis, C. S.   The Everlasting Man 147
Lilja, George   Loving God 148
Littauer, Florence   The Spirit Controlled Temperament 149

The Divine Library 150

Henrietta Mears

Lonie, Don   Things I've Learned 151

Lykins, Don   Fight, Practical Handbook for
Living 152

Charles Malik and Books 153

Markley, Kenneth   The Sovereignty of God 154

Catherine Marshall–Peter Marshall 155

May, Daniel   Tough Times Never Last 156

McBirnie, W. S.   How to Pray 157

McEachern, Jim   Destined for the Throne 158

McFarland, Bob   The Reason Why 159

McGovern, R. Gordon   Ecclesiastes 160

McMillan, R. L.   The Mystery of Godliness 161

Moses Mendelssohnm and Books 162

Miller, Tracy   The Christ Life 163

The Complete Library 164

Charles Haddon Spurgeon

Moore, Sam   A Life of Trust 165

John Mott and Books 166

Executives 167

Mowery, George   Prophet to India

Smith, Donald   The Indescribable Christ

George Mueller and a Book 168

Mueller, John   1980 Countdown to Armageddon 169

Musser, Carolyn   Living Without Losing 170

Narramore, Clyde   The Sensation of Being Somebody 171

Nazigian, Arthur   Spiritual Leadership 172

The Book 173

The Book, by Benjamin Weiss 174

The Bible, the Best, by Cowley 175

Great Americans and the Book: 176

Justice Brewer, Daniel
Webster, Horace Greeley
Patrick Henry and Robert E. Lee
Columbus – Maria von Trapp   177
Presidents and the Bible: 178
Ronald Reagan
John Quincy Adams
Teddy Roosevelt
Woodrow Wilson
John Adams
Billy Graham and the Book   179
Wernher Von Braun and the Book   180
The Book and the Books, by Wilbur Smith   181
A Businessman Looks at the Bible, by W. Maxey Jarman   182
The Bible: Guide for the Businessman, by Marion Wade   183
Booker T. Washington and the Book   184
R. G. Lee and the Book   185
Billy Sunday and the Book   186
Vance Havner and the Book   187
The Right Translation? by C. S. Lewis   188
Early Translations, by Whately   189
Worry Clinic, by George W. Crane, Ph.D., M.D.   190 – 191

Educators and the Book   192

William Lyon Phelps, Robert Coles and McGeorge Bundy

A Book I'd Like to Share   193

Nelson, Warren   Faith Under Fire   194
Niesen, H. Willard   The Saving Life of Christ   195
Ortlund, Raymond   A Spiritual Clinic   196
Owen, G. Frederick   Character Sketches   197
Page, Don   Christianity and History   198
Palmen, Ralph   Here's How to Succeed – Your Money   199
Phillips, Bob   When Caring Is Not Enough   200
Poe, William   Deeper Experiences of Famous Christians   201
Polston, Don   The Law of Faith   202
Prater, Arnold   Rees Howells, Intercessor   203

Great Evangelists and Books   204

John Wesley – George Whitefield

Price, Frederick   The Authority of the Believer   205
Price, Nelson   The Greatest Thing in the World   206
Rawlings, John   Elemental Theology   207

Jim Rayburn and a Book   208

Reaves, C. W.   Adventure of Living   209
Reisinger, Ernest   Pilgrim's Progress   210

Rhode, Naomi	The Agony and the Ecstasy 211
Rickard, Marvin	The Light and the Glory 212
Robertson, Pat	Rees Howell, Intercessor 213
Robinson, Frank Jr.	The Pursuit of God 214
Ross, Doug	Decision Making & the Will of God 215
Rudisill, James	The Christian's Secret of a Happy Life 216
Ryan, Jim	The Pursuit of Holiness 217

Pittsburgh Steelers Bible Study Fellowship   218

Hoff, Hollis	Lectures to My Students
Dungy, Tony	Miraculous Gifts
Long, Terry	Paul Bunyan
Nelson, Edmund	The Lazarus Effect
Shell, Donnie	Seasons of Life
Stallworth, John	Three Steps Forward
Thompson, Weggie	A Hunter's Fireside Book
Webster, Mike	How Come It's Taking Me So Long
Anderson, Gary	Thirty Nine Steps
Campbell, Scott	Treasure Island
Colquitt, Craig	Frankenstein
McJunkin, Kirk	Greatest Success in the World
Toews, Loren	Sand County Almanac
Wolfley, Craig	Instant Replay
Sams, Ron	Encourage Me 219

Mission Directors   220

Saulnier, Harry	Romans Verse by Verse
Hill, Sherburn	The Crises of the Christ
Tabor, Randall	Management for Christian Leader
McMillen, Dick	Making of a Man of God
Scarborough, Luther	Principals of Spiritual Growth 221
Schelling, Gerald	Revival Lectures 222
Semaan, Dick	The Ultimate Power 223
Shoemaker, Sam	The Tragic Sense of Life 224

Professional Baseball   225

Eric Show – Frank Tanana

Schultz, Earl	Master Plan of Evangelism 226
Sir Louis, Vern	What the Bible Teaches 227
Smith, Oswald	Life of David Brainerd 228
Smith, Wilbur	A Man of the Word 229
Sproul, R. C.	The Sermons of Jonathan Edwards 230
Staggs, James	Christian Principles in Business 231
Stanley, Charles	Transformation of the Inner Man 232
Steckel, Kenneth	The Enduement of Power 233
Stedman, Ray	The Problem of Pain 234
Steele, Paul	Balancing the Christian Life 235
Swets, Paul	Man's Search for Meaning 236

Swindoll, Charles   Spiritual Leadership 237
Tam, R. Stanley   Revival Lectures 238

Hudson Taylor and a Booklet 239

Thomas, Cal   True Spirituality 240
Timberlake, Lewis   You're Someone Special 241
Toland, C. E.   The Making of a Christian Leader 242
Toms, Paul   Meditations and Devotions 243
Towns, Elmer   The Christian's Secret of a Happy Life 244
True, Herb   The Imitation of Christ 245
Useldinger, Ron   God Owns My Business 246
Valentine, Paul   Love Made Perfect 247
Vinger, Carl   The Emotions of a Man 248
Wall, Marvin   Where Is God When It Hurts 249
Wallace, Joanne   Birthright. Christian Do You Know Who You Are? 250
Wallace, Tom   The University of Hard Knocks 251
Watson, Draper   Be the Leader You Were Meant to Be 252

Pastors 253-255

Gehman, Bob   The Christian Manifesto
Hodges, Cecil   The Life of Adoniram Judson
Blair, Charles   The Spiritual Man
Monroe, Bill   Holy Spirit, Who He Is, What He Does
Dowhower, Richard   The Denial of Death
Weaver, Luke   How to Live a Victorious Life
Castellani, John   Put God on Main Street
Weitzen, H. Skip   Down to Earth: Laws of Harvest 256
Whitaker, D. F.   12 Ways to Develop a Positive Attitude 257
Wickman, Floyd   Confessions of a Happy Christian 258
Williamson, Jerry   God's Miraculous Plan of Economy 259
Wilson, W. Heartsill   How to Make a Habit of Succeeding 260
Wyrtzen, Jack   Balancing the Christian Life 261

P.J. Zondervan: Books and Reading 262

Great Thoughts on Reading and Study 263

Church Libraries, by Charles Haddon Spurgeon 264
G. Campbell Morgan on Reading 265

Study 266-269

Oswald Chambers—Fulton Sheen
Emmett Fox—John R. Stott
Educators: Robert Milligan—Raymond Muncy 270

Bibliography 271-279

Introduction

Every good thought, every good thing that has happened in my life is related directly or indirectly to a book. That should explain my motivation for this book. If I lived a million years, I could not repay the debt of gratitude I feel for those who invested their lives in writing and the many who thought enough of me to give me a book.

My management training began with a Sunday School class of young boys in 1950. My dear friend, Willard Niesen, gave me a book by Donald Grey Barnhouse. That book helped me enough that the boys were able to give me time to learn to teach.

My early business experience was one failure and discouragement after another. My boss, Bill Meckley, gave me a book by Paul Speicher that fueled my hopes and dreams. One line that I've never forgotten—'An attitude of gratitude flavors everything you do'. I discovered through books that if you keep working and are thankful, success is inevitable.

Each of my children have been a blessing and a challenge. Only through the books we read together, that I gave them, or they discovered, did we weather the storms and become closer rather than drift further apart. Now I'm experiencing the same joy of closeness with my grandchildren through book reading and memorizing incentives.

It was through a severe physical crisis that lasted several months that I began to read with my heart and not just my mind. No drugs could have provided the 'high' of realizing all those wonderful truths that lay dormant in me awaiting words to frame the thoughts so I could think, share, and experience them.

Through books even success took on a different meaning when after exceeding all my financial dreams and pushing forty, I suddenly lost everything. The following years were agonizing, humiliating and frustrating. But because of books, those years became the most wonderful of my life. Books helped me to laugh at heartaches, concentrate on the essential, and be thankful in everything. Authors, Oswald Chambers and Watchman Nee, became my closest friends even though I had never met either one.

And finally my marriage. How wonderful it would be if all our courtship dreams would turn into reality following the marriage. Fortunately for Gloria and me, we were totally committed to each other, but we were still in different worlds. Books changed that too. One of my favorite authors is A.W. Tozer. As Gloria began to enjoy Tozer and many other beautiful books our worlds became one.

I hope the books you discover through this book will enrich your life so tremendously that all who meet you will sense that you are a better person because of the books you've read. As you read remember:

Don't read to be big,
   Read to be down to earth.
Don't read to be smart,
   Read to be real.
Don't read to memorize,
   Read to realize.
Don't read to learn,
   Read to sometimes unlearn.
Don't read a lot,
   Read just enough to keep yourself curious and hungry, to learn more, to keep getting younger as you grow older.

                                        Charles E. Jones

The Love and Power of God Through Books

Except a living man, there is nothing more wonderful than a book!—a message to us from the dead—from human souls whom we never saw, who lived, perhaps, thousands of miles away; and yet these, in those little sheets of paper, speak to us, amuse us, terrify us, teach us, comfort us, open their hearts to us as brothers. . . . I say we ought to reverence books, to look at them as useful and mighty things. If they are good and true, whether they are about religion or politics, farming, trade, or medicine, they are the message of Christ, the maker of all things, the teacher of all truth.

—Kingsley

Kenneth Taylor and a Book

Chairman of the Board, Tyndale House,
Author, The Living Bible

So here you have it: the most important crisis point in your life after believing in Christ as Savior. . . . Will you make Him your Lord and Master and King?

Let me tell you how it happened in my own life. I was brought up in a strong Christian home where God was deeply honored. Our family read the Bible together every day and each one of us prayed. I became a Christian before I can remember – I didn't go through any "rebellious teens." I respected my parents and was glad to try to please them. My college days were happy and reasonably hard working. Perhaps the only unusual thing about them was the fact that it was a Christian school and so there were revival weeks twice a year. I was often challenged to turn over my life to God, and I tried to do this. But as I look back at it now, I realize I was always clutching a few keys to rooms in my life, and not willing to let go and give them to Christ.

So there was progress, but in a stumbling sort of way. I didn't want to let go of things like popularity, or a medical or legal career that would lead to wealth and respect. One thing I especially didn't want to be was a pastor or missionary. I kept those keys in my pocket. As a result, I had a lot of unhappiness and depression and jealousy. God was saying, "Let go. I must have those keys, too." But I was saying, "No!"

It was during the summer of my junior year in college that I let them go. Here is how it happened. I WAS READING A BOOK on a Sunday afternoon. It was a BIOGRAPHY OF BILL BORDEN, a Yale University student many years ago. He was a very unusual man in many ways. He was an excellent student and was on the varsity wrestling team. He was spiritually strong—he used to go down to a city rescue mission (like those the Salvation Army operates) and preach to the alcoholics and other homeless men there, telling them of God's love for them and urging them to let God rescue them and give them useful lives again. But to me, one of the most interesting facts about Bill Borden was that his father had been a millionaire and left his fortune to Bill! How strange to learn that Bill had given it away to missionary societies and other Christian projects, so more people would hear and accept the Good News. Then came an even heavier surprise: Bill decided to become a missionary! Here was this man I had grown to like and respect so much as I read about him, and he was doing two important things exactly opposite to what I was planning. My plans, remember, were never to be a missionary, and to become wealthy. He gave away his money and became a missionary! My conscience was hard hit. I knew I should be willing to do whatever God wanted me to do, and not hold out on these points, or on any others. But I wouldn't do it.

Didn't I realize what a fool I was—to try running my own life when God was willing to run it for me? Yes, but I feared God might not let me have the things I wanted in life. Of course, I was right: He probably wouldn't. For what I wanted was for myself, not for God or others. I faced the problem many others faced then and face now. You may be facing it, too. Who is going to run your life? You, or God? If you decide to run it yourself, you will have half a chance or less of achieving your goals. Hard work with a positive attitude can sometimes work wonders. Sometimes. But if you succeed in getting to the top of the ladder, will it turn out you went to the top of the wrong wall? Probably so. The right place for you is God's will, so it is eternal foolishness to spend your life rushing after your own goals. Eternal, because a judgement day is coming when eternal rewards will be passed out by Christ the King, and it will be true that the first and most important down here may be the least appreciated in heaven – children of God, yes, but coming only with wasted lives to offer Him in shame.

Well, I've gotten ahead of my story. As I read on in the book about Bill Borden, puzzled and dismayed by his decision to let God run his life, I learned that only a few weeks after arriving in Egypt to begin his work as a missionary to the Arab world, he woke up one morning feeling sick, and had to stay in bed with a high fever. The fever didn't go away, but became worse, and it looked very bad, as if he might even die!

Well, I had heard and read enough missionary stories to know how God sometimes heals people, so I was completely unprepared to find out that God didn't heal Bill. Instead, he died. I was utterly shocked. To think – Bill had given everything to God – wealth, opportunity, everything – and still God snuffed out his life.

God was unfair. God was ungrateful. I would never serve a God like that, so I decided then and there to go my own way. I would run my own life instead of entrusting it to God. I turned my back on Him and His safe path, and spiritually stepped over the cliff to plunge to the rocks below.

Then a strange thing happened. God had mercy on me. Even as I was defying Him and deciding to do what I wanted instead of what He wanted, my mind changed and I saw the fatal foolishness of that decision. A moment later, I was down on my knees beside the chair where I had been reading. I found myself praying and telling God that He could have my life, and I would do whatever He wanted me to with it. It was as though He reached out for me as I was going over the cliff, pulled me back, and gave me a second chance. From then on, although there were some bumps along the way when I had relapses and stepped off God's path for my own (and God disciplined me until I came back), I have set my goal: to belong to Him alone and be what He wants me to be, and do what He tells me to. What happiness and joy there has been as a result!

What if I had insisted on going my own way? Well, I might have been reasonably successful for the years down here on earth, but the eternal rewards – that last forever and ever – would be gone, and the joys I experience in living for God in this life would never be.

Here is what the Bible has to say about it:

"All who listen to my instructions," Jesus said, "and follow them, are wise, like a man who builds his house on solid rock. Though the rain comes in torrent, and the floods rise and the storm winds beat against his house, it won't collapse, for it is built on rock.

"But those who hear my instructions and ignore them are foolish, like a man who builds his house on sand. For when the rains and floods come, and storm winds beat against his house, it will fall with a mighty crash." (Matthew 7:24–27)

William Borden and a Book

May 17, 1905

DARLING MOTHER—I am glad that you have told Father about my desire to be a missionary. I am thinking about it all the time, and looking forward to it with a good deal of anticipation. I know that I am not at all fitted out or prepared yet, but in the next four or five years I ought to be able to prepare myself. I have been reading Mr. Speer's book on *Missionary Principles and Practice*. It is very good, in my opinion. You may have read it, and if you haven't I think you would like it.

June 4, 1905

I have just finished reading Mr. Speer's book. It has helped me a great deal. I especially noticed the two chapters he takes to the Student Volunteer Movement. He shows very clearly what the motto, "The Evangelization of the World in this Generation" means, and how perfectly possible it is, provided we pray the Lord of the harvest to send forth labourers. There is something inspiring in the project to me. It is something fine, something worth every effort to accomplish and which will repay us when we have done our duty.

When I got through reading, I knelt right down and prayed more earnestly than I have for some time for the mission work and for God's plan for my life, and also for His plans for the lives of every one of my family. Oh, Mother, do pray for me. College is so near and there will be such a lot of things to do, tremendous opportunities! Pray that I may be guided in everything, small and great.

The Blessed Library
Bishop Joseph Hall

What a world of thought is here packed up together! I know not whether this sight doth more dismay or comfort me. It dismays me to think that here is so much that I cannot know; it comforts me to think that this variety affords so much assistance to know what I should. . . . What a happiness is it that, without the aid of necromancy, I can here call up any of the ancient worthies of learning, whether human or divine, and confer with them upon all my doubts; that I can at pleasure summon whole synods of reverend fathers and acute doctors from all the coasts of the earth, to give their well-studied judgments in all doubtful points which I propose. Nor can I cast my eye casually upon any of these silent masters but I must learn somewhat. It is a wantonness to complain of choice. No law binds us to read all; but the more we can take in and digest, the greater will be our improvement.

Blessed be God who hath set up so many clear lamps in his church: none but the wilfully blind can plead darkness. And blessed be the memory of those, his faithful servants, who have left their blood, their spirits, their lives, in these precious papers; and have willingly wasted themselves into these enduring monuments to give light to others.

Chuck Colson and a Book

President, Fellowship Communications

One hot summer night in August of 1973 I visited an old friend at his home outside of Boston. It was during the darkest days of Watergate. My whole world was being turned upside down.

My friend was a keen businessman who had worked his way to the top. President of one of the largest corporations in America in his early forties, he was a hard-charging man driven to succeed. I understood – I was just like him.

But when I had paid him a quick visit during a business trip several months earlier, I had been astonished to find him peaceful, calm: dramatically different.

When I asked him about it, he answered with an extraordinary explanation: "I have accepted Jesus Christ." I had never heard anything like those words before; but I could not deny he had changed.

This August night, though I couldn't admit it to anyone, I was seeking something. I knew my friend might have an answer. Something was wrong in my own life. Something much more than Watergate; I was empty inside, groping for whatever meaning there was to life, if indeed there was any.

That night he told me about his encounter with Jesus Christ, how his life had been transformed. Then he picked up a paperback book off a coffee table, opened it to a chapter titled "Pride," and began to read.

It was one of the most extraordinary moments of my life. The words from that book – *Mere Christianity* – ripped through the protective armor in which I had unknowingly encased myself for 41 years. Lewis wrote about man's great sin – his pride – as a spiritual cancer.

The events of my own life flashed before me. I thought I had been driven by a desire to provide for my family, build a good law firm, serve my country. But in reality what I was doing all those years was feeding my pride, proving how good I was. Lewis convinced me that all my efforts had been in vain, that in my drive for the top I had missed the real pinnacle – to know God in a personal way.

As I left my friend's home that night, I accepted his gift of the copy of *Mere Christianity*. I was deeply moved by his testimony and by the chapter he had read – though I refused to show it. But as I got into my car, the White House tough guy – the hatchet-man, or so the press called me – crumbled in a flood of tears, unable to drive, calling out to God with the first honest prayer of my life. That was the night Jesus Christ came into my life.

Over the next week, I studied *Mere Christianity*. I underlined, made notes, even kept a yellow pad at my side with two columns – one headed "there is a God," the other headed "there is not a God." On another sheet of paper I had two more columns – "Jesus Christ is God" – "Jesus Christ is not God."

I read the book as if I was studying for the most important case I had ever argued. Lewis' logic was so utterly compelling that I was left with no recourse but to accept the reality of God Who is and Who has revealed Himself through Jesus Christ. *Mere Christianity* simply sets forth a powerful, rational case for the Christian faith in a wonderfully readable way.

Since then I have given out hundreds of copies of *Mere Christianity* and have met hundreds whose lives have been transformed by it. It is the book God has used most powerfully in my life, apart from His own Word.

But I must warn you, it is not a book you can pick up and put down easily, nor is it a book you can read and remain the same person as before. For it masterfully presents the case for Christ. After reading it, the uncommitted person can only make a choice for or against Him.

That is the most important decision one ever faces. For the answer determines one's eternal destiny and the meaning of life.

Bert Decker and a Book

President Decker Communications

Seven years ago I was headed out the door for one of my routine trips to the East Coast when my wife thrust a book into my hand, urging me to read it. One glance at the title was enough to sour me; I had no affection for the Nixon administration, especially the hatchet man who had gone religious. I wasn't much interested in God, either. But my wife said it was a "powerful book," so my curiosity was aroused. I figured there'd be some redeeming political insights at least.

Little did I imagine that an hour into the flight, I'd find tears streaming down my face as Colson discovered his immense pride, quoting from C. S. Lewis' *Mere Christianity:*

> In God you come up against something which is in every respect immeasurably superior to yourself. Unless you know God as that – and, therefore, know yourself as nothing in comparison – you do not know God at all. As long as you are proud you cannot know God. A proud man is always looking down on things and people; and, of course, as long as you are looking down, you cannot see something that is above you.

I wish someday I could thank him in person for writing *Born Again.* Thousands of others probably wish the same thing.

John Newton and Thomas à Kempis

It was in 1742 that he met Mary Catlett, daughter of his mother's greatest friend and at the time fourteen years of age. The same year found him making an acquaintance with Shaftesbury by reading his *Characteristics*. Because of the influence of this book, John Newton became an infidel . . .

In February, 1747, he was freed from a captivity of about fifteen months. It was on his return voyage, on a boat which had spent months in the gathering of gold, ivory, dyers' wood, and beeswax, that he picked up a copy of *Thomas à Kempis*.

"I carelessly picked it up," he wrote, "as I had often done before, to pass away the time; but I had still read it with the same indifference as if it were entirely a romance. However, while I was reading this time, an involuntary suggestion arose in my mind. What if these things should be true? I could not bear the weight of the inference, as it related to myself, and therefore shut the book presently. My conscience witnessed against me once more; and I concluded that, true or false, I must abide the consequences of my own choice. . . ."

It was on March 21, 1748, at the age of twenty-three, that Newton sought the mercy of God.

—William Culbertson

David Livingstone 1813–1873
The Right Book at the Right Time

David Livingstone was not fond of religious reading, and he tells us, with that quiet humor which never deserted him, that his last flogging was received for refusing to read Wilberforce's *Practical Christianity.* This dislike continued for years, until he discovered Dick's *Philosophy of Religion,* and *Philosophy of a Future State,* which he found to his delight enforced his own conviction that religion and science were friendly to each other. It was while reading *Philosophy of Religion* and *Philosophy of a Future State* that he became convinced that it was his duty and highest privilege to accept Christ's salvation for himself. This was in his twentieth year. He had many earnest thoughts about religion for years, but only now did the great spiritual change occur. "This change," he says, "was like what may be supposed would take place were it possible to cure a case of 'color-blindness'." The fullness with which the pardon of all our guilt is offered in God's Book drew forth feelings of affectionate love to Him who bought us with His blood, which in some small measure has influenced my conduct ever since. Although at first he had no thought of becoming a missionary himself, he made a resolution that, as the salvation of men ought to be the chief aim of every Christian, he would give missions all that he could earn beyond what was required for his subsistence. It was about a year later that, after reading Dr. Gutzlaff's "Appeal" on behalf of China, he resolved to give himself to the work in that country.

Jonathan Edwards and Books

His eagerness to read widely was not the quest for knowledge alone. It was the pursuit of new insights and interpretations concerning the supreme revelation of truth in Jesus Christ. To Edwards all the treasures of wisdom and knowledge were found in Christ. His readings and meditation were centered in Christ as the alpha and the omega. The aim of the hours given to study was the enlargement of spiritual knowledge. Out of the glory of that lighted mind, Edwards ministered to his people without narrowness or limitation. From many sources Edwards fed the springs of inspiration. Reading made Edwards "a full man."

Those who have imagined that Edwards was a man of few books in an out-of-the-way place are mistaken in their estimate of him. He was in touch with the best literature of that period by private purchase or by loan from his friends. If his library could not be measured as large in terms of what is available today, it had depth and stimulus within the ambit of a mind ever open to the insights of all schools of thought.

This *Catalogue* of reading is an extremely interesting document. Therein we catch a glimpse of the methods of the preacher preparing himself for his task. As a commonplace book the *Catalogue* served as a sourcebook and a thesaurus of mental and spiritual stimulus. No examination of Edwards' development as a preacher can dismiss this powerful influence upon him in his habit and discipline. In this way he conserved the best that was written and became acquainted with the most helpful books of that day. Especially was this true of the Puritan writings to which he pays tribute again and again.

David Brainerd and Jonathan Edwards

So completely did Edward's life dominate Brainerd's that it is necessary to know the former if the latter is to be understood. Spurgeon so admired Puritan theology that his ultimate title seems best expressed in the shadow of the broad brim. But that influence came from a great company of men; it left Mr. Spurgeon free to develop a personality of his own. However, with Brainerd – if ever any single man, in due subordination to Christ, was permitted to be another's ideal – that's what Edwards became to Brainerd. In fact, he out-Edwardsed Edwards. Edwards admired the life of self-effacement; Brainerd put a magnifying glass on Edwards' admiration – and lived it!

So, we give you Jonathan Edwards (Oct. 5, 1703–March 22, 1758), whose career first shaped, and then whose eyes affectionately interpreted, the short, pathetic life of his counterpart, David Brainerd.

It is striking that Brainerd, when twenty-two and already an avid reader of Edwards, had the same experience. More striking still, that when the Indians at Crossweeksung became Christians their account of it was just like Brainerd's. "Not think anything 'bout self: Just how good God is." Thus the Indians became, in effect, theological grandchildren of Edwards.

"Heaven and earth shall pass away, but my words shall not pass away."
– Matthew 24:35

A BOOK
I'D LIKE
TO SHARE

Nothing ought to be more weighed than the nature of books recommended by public authority. So recommended, they soon form the character of the age. Uncertain indeed is the efficacy, limited indeed is the extent, of a virtuous institution. But if education takes in *vice* as any part of its system, there is no doubt but that it will operate with abundant energy, and to an extent indefinite.

—Burke

College Presidents

A Catalogue of Sins

by William May
Recommended by: Mark W. Lee,
President, Simpson College

I find it difficult to select only one title, as so many have meant a great deal to me. There are several vital authors, but I will choose William May's, *A Catalogue of Sins.*

May's ideas are insightful in showing a "surplus of grace" in all the problems of man. May shows that surplus in apocalypse, worship, and ethics, but especially in comedy.

Spiritual Leadership

by J. Oswald Sanders
Recommended by: Dr. Stuart Lease,
Former President, Lancaster Bible College

Among the many books which helped, guided and encouraged me while I was President of Lancaster Bible College, I found a book entitled *Spiritual Leadership* by J. Oswald Sanders especially profitable. At the time of writing it, he was General Director of the Overseas Missionary Fellowship (formerly known as the China Inland Mission and now known as OMF International).

Spiritual Leadership is a book that helps to build up leaders so that they in turn can build up others. It's great to be involved in this process of edification!

College Presidents

He that Is Spiritual

by Lewis Chafer
Recommended by: John Walword,
President, Dallas Theological Seminary

Imitation of Christ

by Thomas à Kempis
Recommended by D. Ray Hostetter
President, Messiah College

Mystery of Marriage

by Mike Mason
Recommended by Joe Aldrich
President, Multnomah School
of The Bible

Through the Valley of the Kwai

by Ernest Gordon
Recommended by: Hudson T. Armerding,
Former President, Wheaton College

Ernest Gordon's book, *Through the Valley of the Kwai,* tells how an enlisted man asked him to read the Bible to him. This was after they both had been terribly mistreated by the Japanese. In fact I wept as I read about what happened when a shovel was missing. The Japanese officer asked who stole it, but no one responded. Then they were all threatened with severe punishment. At that, one man stepped forward and said that he would take the blame for the loss. Before them all, the Japanese officer beat him to death. Later, the shovel was found. The man really was innocent but because he believed the Bible taught that one should lay down his life for his friends, he took the penalty.

This was typical of the change that occurred as Gordon and the others sought to follow what Scripture taught. When a trainload of Japanese wounded came in to the station alongside their train, some British soldiers who had been horribly mistreated by the enemy went over and ministered to the Japanese wounded, because they believed that this was what God wanted them to do. Gordon found that obedience to Scripture's commands can bring about a dramatic change in our attitudes and practices . . .

This is what the manner of life of the Christian leader should be. It should manifest a conformity to the teachings of the Word of God. And it should reflect the indwelling presence and power of the Holy Spirit as he both discloses the will of God and enables the believer to do it.

—Excerpts from *Leadership*
Tyndale House Publishers

The Law of Faith

by Norman Grubb
Recommended by: Robert A. Cook,
President, King's College

A book that has been used in my life is *The Law of Faith*.

The striking fact is that normally these men of God (Moses and Elisha) took the supply of God for a sudden emergency in their stride, as it were. They took it for granted that where need was, there also was divine supply, if they would simply draw on it. Look at Elisha providing the oil, healing the fountain, raising the axe-head, getting the water for the army, and so on. But what was special revelation to them is meant to be common grace to us, "the mystery which hath been hid from ages and from generations but now is made manifest to His saints . . . which is Christ in you." The life in Christ is not to be regarded as a life lived by jerks, sometimes in and sometimes out of His will.

What we learn from Moses and Elisha, and from Jesus the Son of Man, is that, unless we are consciously opposed to God in heart, the supply of our daily needs is His will; such indeed is the meaning of the prayer for our daily bread. Just where we are is God's plan for us, and just what we need where we are is what God would give us. Our environment is our opportunity. Our environment provides both the material and justification for boldness of faith. All that Moses or Elisha, or the Lord Himself, did was to meet the sudden next need of daily life with a taking-for-granted faith that the Father would supply, and a declaration of that faith, and such action as was the natural consequence of such faith.

There you have it. One of the great secrets of spiritual life and power.

Strategy for Living

by Edward Dayton and Ted Engstrom
Recommended by: Pierre Guillermin,
President, Liberty University

As Christians we are given a mandate by God to Biblical stewardship of all that we have and all that we are: material possessions, talents and abilities, time, relationships – every area of our lives. We are not compartmentalized beings who can shut off or shut out selected areas of our lives. And so it becomes incumbent upon us to develop a Christian strategy for living wisely and productively.

Strategy for Living, by Edward Dayton and Ted Engstrom, addresses effective life management in an insightful, pragmatic and highly readable style:

"Each one of us has been given responsibility for himself. Each one of us is an individual before God. Each one of us has all the gifts that God meant us to have. In the many different roles that we play, in the many different situations of life that we face, under the many demands that are placed upon us, we are faced with ourselves, managing our lives, finding a strategy to live by."

This book provides simple yet profound guidelines for becoming responsible stewards of our lives of whom He will say one day, "Well done, thou good and faithful servant. . . ."

The Battle for The Bible

by Harold Lindsell
Recommended by: W. D. Hungerpiller, President,
Carver Bible Institute and College—Atlanta, Ga.

The Battle for The Bible is a must for any Christian worker who plans to serve the Lord as pastor, missionary, or in any other spiritual endeavor in which he or she will influence others. Lindsell's evaluation of the erosion that has taken place in many denominations and theological schools, relative to the inerrancy of the Scriptures, should strike a chord of concern and exhortation to contend for the faith, lest we find ourselves with no sure word of prophecy. If the foundation be destroyed, which is the Word of God, we become like a ship without a rudder in a turbulent sea. To use the proverbial saying, "putting our heads in the sand like an ostrich," hoping that the problem will go away and acting as if the problem does not exist, is fantasy. This is a plea to return to the full, verbal inspiration of the Bible:

"Of all the doctrines connected with the Christian faith, none is more important than the one that has to do with the basis of our religious knowledge. For anyone who professes the Christian faith the root question is: From where do I get my knowledge on which my faith is based? The answers to this question are varied, of course, but for the Christian at least it always comes full circle to the Bible. When all has been said and done the only true and dependable source for Christianity lies in the book we call the Bible. This is the presupposition for which I start. . . ."

The Knowledge of the Holy

by A.W. Tozer
Recommended by: William J. McRae,
President, Ontario Theological Seminary

"What comes into our minds when we think about God is the most important thing about us."

With these words, Tozer begins what has become the most influential book, apart from the Scriptures, in my life. It exposed my greatest deficiency, created an insatiable thirst for the knowledge of God, and prodded me in my pursuit of Him.

"A right conception of God is basic not only to systematic theology but to practical Christian living as well. It is to worship what the foundation is to the temple; where it is inadequate or out of plumb the whole structure must sooner or later collapse. I believe there is scarcely an error in doctrine or a failure in applying Christian ethics that cannot be traced finally to imperfect or ignoble thoughts about God."

Show me a person's priorities, personal life, and future plans, and I will tell you what he thinks of God! How we cope with crises, face temptations, handle money, and deal with anxiety is significantly influenced by our concept of God.

"It is my opinion that the Christian conception of God current in these middle years of the twentieth century is so decadent as to be utterly beneath the dignity of the Most High God and actually constitutes for professed believers something amounting to a moral calamity."

Tozer has introduced me to the attributes of God – a subject that has not only consumed many of my study and devotional hours for several years but has become my favourite topic for preaching. Here is the soil in which my spirit has been nurtured.

"Let him that glorieth glory in this, that he understandeth and knoweth Me." (Jeremiah 9:24a)

Bush Aglow

by Richard Elsworth Day
Recommended by: George Sweeting,
President, Moody Bible Institute

The book that influenced me most in my early life is *Bush Aglow*, the life story of D. L. Moody. As to why this book influenced me, I thought, "If God could use D. L. Moody with all of his limitations, then there is hope for me."

President H. G. Weston, of the Crozer Theological Seminary followed Dr. Scofield. In closing a beautiful tribute to his friend, he said:
"I count as one of the greatest blessings of my life my acquaintance with Mr. Moody, the influence he has had on me, and the privilege of studying God's methods in his life and work. He was the greatest religious character of this century. We instinctively attribute the success of every man who is eminent in attracting and influencing others to some special natural endowment, to education and training, or to a peculiar magnetic personality. Mr. Moody had none of these; yet no man has surpassed him in his power of attraction and influence, both over masses of men and over individuals of strong character, of executive ability, of great resources, whom he fastened to himself with hooks of steel, making them not only his life-long friends, but his constant partners in all his good works. This marvellous power, wielded for so many years, undiminished to the end, we cannot explain by any one peculiar natural gift. He had none of them.

"What had He? He had life. I do not mean the manner of living, but what the Bible means by this word — what Christ means when He declares the purpose of His coming: 'I am come that they might have life, and that they might have it more abundantly.'"

Your God Is Too Small

by J. B. Phillips
Recommended by: Bill Williams,
President, Grand Canyon College

Your God Is Too Small provides insight for viewing the majesty, magnificence and magnitude of God. The subtle manner in which we limit God in our thinking process of language consideration, cultural consideration and many other factors really can deprive us of the fullest appreciation of God's greatness.

By focusing our thoughts towards the unbounded love and limitless power, we draw strength for our Christian walk by a much higher appreciation of God's redeeming work and love:

"We can never have too big a conception of God, and the more scientific knowledge (in whatever field) advances, the greater becomes our idea of His vast and complicated wisdom. Yet, unless we are to remain befogged and bewildered and give up all hope of ever knowing God as a Person, we have to accept His own planned focusing of Himself in a human being, Jesus Christ.

"If we accept this as fact, as *the* Fact of history, it becomes possible to find a satisfactory and comprehensive answer to a great many problems, and, what is equally important, a reasonable shelf on which the unsolved perplexities may be left with every confidence."

The Presence of the Kingdom

by Jacques Ellul
Recommended by: Jay Kesler, President,
Taylor University

I constantly struggle with the role of the common man in the work of Christ and always felt that the answers given, such as to win souls, or to be a good churchman, or to live a spiritual life, were simply not comprehensive enough. I am appalled that oftentimes the man who is literally affecting the lives of hundreds of people through his profession is given the task in the church of teaching junior high boys or giving money or taking up the offering.

I had searched for 15 years as a Christian for a truly comprehensive discussion of the role of the Christian in the modern world until I ran across Jacques Ellul's *The Presence of the Kingdom.* Ellul helps us to understand that the kingdom of God is not only to be understood in terms of the past as introduced by Jesus and His miracles in the New Testament, nor is it to be understood exclusively as something in the future related in some way to going to heaven, but that we live presently as citizens of the kingdom. He discusses man's role as salt, light and sheep among wolves. Ellul helps us to understand man as an end rather than a means to an end as part of the political, industrial, social and even ecclesiastical machinery of the world. He helps us to understand how to function in a fallen world without dividing our minds into sacred secular compartments and, above all, teaches us to appropriate grace as we participate in a real world doing real things that are important to the kingdom of God.

In short, he explains where we are in a technological society, the illusions that surround us and elevates our activity beyond mere "wheel turning" to the dignity that God intended when He created us.

Authentic Christianity

by Ray C. Stedman
Recommended by: Ronald A. Jenson,
Pres., International School of Theology

The book that has had the most constant and deep impact in my life is the book *Authentic Christianity* by Ray C. Stedman. In a day of incredible phoniness and facades, Ray Stedman does a tremendous exposition of II Corinthians 2:14-6:13 as a model for discerning the pale imitation of Christianity from the real thing.

His book helped me to understand the difference between phoniness and genuine expressions of faith. It spoke particularly to the area of integrity and the vitality of Christian life and ministry.

One of his best chapters delineates the five marks of a radical (real) Christian life. This life is characterized by:

1. unquenchable optimism
2. unvarying success
3. unforgetable impact
4. unimpeachable integrity
5. undeniable reality

These five qualities, as well as other pithy insights from his book, have sustained me over the years and served as a benchmark for my Christian growth. I will be forever thankful to Ray Stedman for his fine dealing with a passage of scripture that lays down some of the best guidance anyone can have with reference to committed Christian living.

The Treasury of Scripture Knowledge

by R. A. Torrey
Recommended by: John MacArthur, Jr.,
President, The Master's College

A book that has influenced my life is *The Treasury of Scripture Knowledge.*

Perhaps the best statement that can be made about it is the one by R. A. Torrey which appears in the introduction of the book:

"There is no other commentary on the Bible so helpful as the Bible itself. There is not a difficult passage in the Bible that is not explained and made clear by other passages of the Bible, and this book is marvelously useful in bringing to light those other parts of the Bible that throw light upon the portion that is being studied. But not only does the book illuminate dark places, it also emphasizes the truth by bringing in a multitude of witnesses. It also greatly strengthens faith, for one cannot study his Bible with the aid of *The Treasury of Scripture Knowledge* without getting a deeper conviction of the unity of the entire Book. As he compares Scripture with Scripture and sees how what Paul says fits in to what Jesus said, and John said, and Peter said, and Isaiah said, and the Psalmist said; when he sees how every doctrine of the New Testament regarding Christ, His Divine-human nature, His holy character, His atoning death, and His resurrection, ascension, and coming again is enfolded in the types of the Pentateuch, Prophets, and Psalms, he becomes overwhelmingly convinced that the whole Bible has one real Author behind the many human authors. *The Treasury of Scripture Knowledge* enables one, not only to understand the Word, but to feed upon the Word."

For the word of God is quick, and powerful,
and sharper than any two-edged sword.
—*Heb. 4:12*

The Problem of Pain

by C. S. Lewis
Recommended by: Rev. Buford Adams,
Pastor, Morrow, Georgia

One of the most basic questions of life is answered with clear thinking and real scholarship.

Sooner or later everyone will face a situation that seems absolutely mindless and unfair. We lose a loved one. We are brutalized by a criminal or victimized by bureaucracy. We see children helpless in the face of war or starvation. None of the standard answers give hope. If there is no God or if God is Himself evil or impotent, then we are cast upon an uncertain sea indeed.

Lewis explains that the very basis of Christianity is faith and faith involves two fundamental conclusions. First, God is . . . that is, He does exist and He is in control. Second, God loves. How then do we explain suffering? If God is and God loves, why does He allow unfair suffering?

The answer lies in the fact that God has allowed us freedom to choose good or evil and real freedom always carries with it the potential for wrong decisions and wrong results. The truth is we have the best world we can have given our freedom. Even so, God's heart of love has and is making provision to correct the evil by paying the price Himself in His Son.

It is not often that such a universally troubling subject is dealt with so effectively. The man or woman who wants real answers and is willing to think clearly will find *The Problem of Pain* an honest comfort.

I am the bread of life; he that cometh to me shall never hunger; and he that believeth on me shall never thirst.

—John 6:35

Evangelism and
the Sovereignty of God

by J. I. Packer
Recommended by: William L. Austin,
Pastor, Orlando, Florida

The book has meant a great deal to me, and I have given away many copies to fellow pastors and Bible College students. In each case those to whom it has been given have found it to be very helpful.

The fact that God is sovereign in all of His works – including salvation – is clearly taught in the Scriptures of the Old as well as the New Testament. It also seems apparent that man in his fallen state is responsible for all his actions. These two truths, God's sovereignty and man's responsibility, seem to have confused many in our day; especially when we face the task of evangelism. There exists today therefore, a widespread suspicion among some evangelicals that any deep commitment to the absolute sovereignty of God will surely undermine any proper sense of human responsibility. Dr. J. I. Packer, in a very clear and Biblical way shows us in *Evangelism and the Sovereignty of God* that such is not the case. He argues most convincingly that far from hindering evangelism, commitment to the sovereignty of God's government and grace is the only thing that can Biblically sustain evangelism when the going gets tough, and resistance mounts.

This is done, in part by Dr. Packer's use and explanation of a spiritual antinomy; that which the Shorter Oxford Dictionary defines as: "a contradiction between conclusions which seem equally logical, reasonable or necessary." An antinomy exists when a pair of principals stand side by side, seemingly irreconcilable, yet both undeniable. A clear understanding of this book will do much to bring both our methods and our message in evangelism back to a more Biblical position.

The Life of Missionary
C. T. Studd

by Norman Grubb
Recommended by: A. A. Baker,
Vice President, Pensacola Christian College

C. T. Studd was one of England's greatest sports heroes. An All-England cricketer, he was considered by many to be as good as any athlete that ever played the game. And yet his athletic accomplishments appear neglible in the light of his missionary service that he gave to his Lord and Savior Jesus Christ.

Consider C. T. Studd the young man on the mission field of China who gave away an inherited fortune so that he would trust the heavenly Father to supply his needs.

Consider C. T. Studd who, after a lifetime on the mission fields of China and India, and at the age of 52, pioneered missionary work in the heart of Africa.

Consider C. T. Studd who was told by his doctor and his mission board that his health was too bad and that he would not survive in tropical Africa. Yet he went and stayed 20 years.

"My only joys therefore are that when God has given me a work to do, I have not refused it."
—C. T. Studd, a blessing to my life.

Ask, and it shall be given you; seek, and ye shall find; knock, and it shall be opened unto you: For every one that asketh receiveth; and he that seeketh findeth; and to him that knocketh it shall be opened.
—*Matthew 7:7, 8*

The Sermon on the Mount

by Emmet Fox
Recommended by: Joe Batten, CPAE, Chairman,
Batten, Batten, Hudson & Swab, Inc.

My introduction to what I consider the finest book this side of the *Holy Bible* occurred in Chicago in November of 1965. I had just wound up a day-long seminar on "Tough-Minded Management" which had been sponsored by the Management Center of Cambridge and the last person to approach me as the others filed out was a bright guy with a big grin.

He said that many of the truths, insights, and techniques reminded him so much of a book entitled, *The Sermon on the Mount*, by Emmet Fox; that he was sure I must have read it many times. I had to confess that I had not even heard of it. He said, "I'll send you a copy." I thanked him and had almost forgotten the promise when the book arrived in the mail.

It is virtually a sublime combination of truth, clarity, practicality, and profundity. I carried it in my briefcase wherever I traveled for over six years and literally wore my original copy out from repeated readings, scribblings, and hands-on usage.

All kinds of beautiful insights and emotional and spiritual vistas seemed to open up to me. I began to refer to Christ as the toughest-minded person ever to walk the earth. I discovered that the word "meek" in the great be-attitude meant tough-minded and had nothing to do with a Milquetoast kind of thing. I learned things about faith, hope, love, gratitude, and forgiveness that literally turned my life around.

Strong's Exhaustive Concordance

Edited by James Strong
Recommended by: Dr. J. Sidlow Baxter,
Author & Bible Teacher

I find it too difficult to pick out just one book for supreme mention. At least twenty have outstandingly influenced me. All knowledge is useful; some is important; but there is one book, one only, a knowledge of which is *vital:* the Bible. If I could have only one book besides the Bible, it would be *Strong's Exhaustive Concordance.* No other can substitute it, not even Young's. I have learned more through it as to what the Bible really teaches than from all the other publications I ever possessed. True to its title, it is indeed "exhaustive." It gives every occurrence of every word, right down to pronouns and monosyllables. Each one is given a number which connects it to a lexicon giving the Hebrew or Greek word and its meaning, and every other English word by which it is translated, enabling our research to be truly "exhaustive." It is based on the King James Version, but it has a "comparative" section showing all places where the English and American revised versions translate differently — and more besides. It can be utilized by those who know no Hebrew or Greek whatever. My own twenty-five books owe more to Strong's than to any other publication.

He was wounded for our transgressions, he was bruised for our iniquities: the chastisement of our peace was upon him; and with his stripes we are healed.

—Isaiah 53:5

The Works of the Mind

by Robert B. Heywood
Recommended by: Joseph Bayly,
Author, Vice President of
David C. Cook Publishing Co.

Books are like friends who meet a certain need at a certain time in your life, then move on. Or you move on.

A few are lifelong: you pick up the friendship at intervals and freshly impressed with the contribution they make to your thought and life.

A secular book was important in my forties. Secular? No, I think God is hidden on just about every page. *The Works of the Mind* brings together, through the brilliant editing of the University of Chicago's Robert B. Heywood, insights on work and creativity by an artist (Marc Chagall), a sculptor (Alfeo Faggi), an architect (Frank Lloyd Wright), a musician (Arnold Schonberg), and eight others in more mundane pursuits. The book stimulated my creative juices as no other book or person has. I keep referring back to it. (A similar book is Strunk and White's *Elements of Style.*)

Trust in the Lord with all thine heart; and lean not unto thine own understanding. In all thy ways acknowledge Him, and He shall direct thy paths.

—Proverbs 3:5,6

Hudson Taylor's Spiritual Secret

by Howard Taylor
Recommended by: Dr. Wally Beebe,
Missionary-Evangelist

Here is a biography (and I like those best) that starts with the life of a young man before he trusts Christ as Saviour. We see what kind of fiber he was made of, similar to many of our own lives. We then see the transformation and the change of direction that comes into this young life and some fascinating, unusual, and unique goals he set in his life before the age of twenty-five. We trace the life of a real man who lived in a real country and who dealt with real people in some of the most adverse circumstances:

"Hudson Taylor was no recluse. He was a man of affairs, the father of a family, and one who bore large responsibilities. Intensely practical, he lived a life of constant change among all sorts and conditions of men. He was no giant in strength, no atlas to bear the world upon his shoulders. Small in stature and far from being strong, he had always to face physical limitations. Next to godly parentage, the chief advantage of his early years was that he had to support himself from the time he was about sixteen. He became a hard worker and an efficient medical man; he was able to care for a baby, cook a dinner, keep accounts, and comfort the sick and sorrowing, no less than to originate great enterprises and afford spiritual leadership to thoughtful men and women the wide world over."

I guarantee you that reading this book will set a perspective in your life, a dedication to task, as never before. The so-called "burned-out Christian worker" will find the answer to that burn-out in this book. Here is the key that, if used, could open to the reader a whole new way of life.

Extraordinary Living
for Ordinary Man

by Sam Shoemaker 1890–1963
Recommended by: Jacob M. Bellig,
Pastor, Castro Valley, California

We have a church family of approximately 4,000 families. We have people from all different backgrounds coming for counseling, and I have found that it is very helpful in these sessions to recommend to them reading material.

Of course, the first book I insist that they read regularly is the Bible and I have a schedule of reading that I recommend so that it is a continuing program. There are additional books that I also suggest, and one of the most helpful has been *Extraordinary Living for Ordinary Man*. I realize that people retain a certain percentage of all that they hear, but they retain a much greater percentage of what they read. Therefore, the establishing of a proper library is very important for everyone.

'Doubt of any sort cannot be removed except by action.' Not much will happen when you remain on dead center – get off dead center, and follow the line of the best – light you have. Do the obvious right thing, and then God can lead you to the inspired thing. Get in motion. You can't guide a bicycle leaning against a wall – you can only guide a bicycle that is in motion. God cannot guide a person who always stands still, paralyzed by doubt and misgiving. Better step out and make a mistake, and really get in motion – then God can get at you to correct the mistake.
—Carlyle

Communications: Key to Your Marriage

by Norman Wright
Recommended by: Peter Bergen,
Pastor, Columbia Falls, Montana

The author gives practical principles for building self-esteem through respect and understanding. "A key to communication is building your mate's self-esteem. A person's self-esteem is his overall judgment of himself. High self-esteem means you have solid feelings of self-respect and self-worth. You are glad you are you."

I have found this statement from Wright to be so true, that "Marriage partners with high self-esteem are bound to be happier and communicate better. High self-esteem means an absence or at least a considerable lessening of anxieties, complexes and the other problems that prevent good communication."

I like his simple yet super definition of communication. That it is "a process (either verbal or nonverbal) of sharing information with another person in such a way that he understands what you are saying. Talking and listening and understanding are all involved in the process of communication."

This outstanding book also gets into:

How to deal with marital conflict,
Ten methods for handling angry feelings,
Ten steps to avoid the high cost of anxiety and worry,
Marriage: The only game both players can win!
What is a "Christian" marriage? Wright says, "Marriage is the total commitment of the total person for the total life."

It's an experience in learning, sharing and communicating.

The Compassionate Touch

by Doug Wead
Recommended by: Bernie Berman,
Executive, Concert Violinist

This is a book that should be read and present in the personal library of everyone who wishes to understand and communicate faith, love and loyalty, and to possess a little of "The Compassionate Touch":

"Calcutta is a city of animals. Thousands of skinny pye-dogs with rabid blood roam lazily through the streets, competing with homeless children for scraps of food. Rats, which outnumber people eight to one, have become increasingly bold. . . . 'The hospital will no longer admit patients without a cat.' Mostly, Calcutta is people – all kinds of people, eight million of them. People with hollow eyes and consumptive coughs. In the bustees, the sprawling slums of Calcutta, live the poorest people on earth. . . . Some know they are poor. . . . But most are ignorant of how poor they are. They have known no other life. The old Indian aristocracy is right. Many of them are happy. . . . Those who are happy, are happy in spite of their poverty, not because of it. . . . There are stories in these bustees, thousands of horrible stories. . . . But there are good stories in Calcutta, too – even in the bustees. . . . These are small lights in a morass of darkness and corruption. They are small, but they are not insignificant. . . . This book is about one of those lights from Calcutta. A mysterious and provocative man, he has appeared out of nowhere, a phantom angel to thousands of homeless children and crippled beggars. . . . He is a white man, which makes his story all the more unlikely. . . . I heard his beautiful, paradoxical story from successful men in suits who came out of bustees. I heard it from crippled children who now can walk. I heard it a hundred times, and it will haunt me for the rest of my life."

The Knowledge of the Holy

by A. W. Tozer
Recommended by: Dan Betzer,
Radio Evangelist

Many books have influenced my life. One of the chief volumes is one with which I am sure many people are familiar, *The Knowledge of the Holy,* by A. W. Tozer, published by Christian Publications, Inc.

In the very first chapter, Dr. Tozer emphasizes the importance of proper knowledge of God:

"Without doubt, the mightiest thought the mind can entertain is the thought of God, and the weightiest word in any language is its word for God. Thought and speech are God's gifts to creatures made in His image; these are intimately associated with Him and impossible apart from Him. It is highly significant that the first word was the Word: 'And the word was with God, and the Word was God.' We may speak because God spoke. In Him word and idea are indivisible.

"That our idea of God correspond as nearly as possible to the true being of God is of immense importance to us. Compared with our actual thoughts about Him, our creedal statements are of little consequence. Our real idea of God may lie buried under the rubbish of conventional religious notions and may require an intelligent and vigorous search before it is finally unearthed and exposed for what it is. Only after an ordeal of painful self-probing are we likely to discover what we actually believe about God."

"The day is thine, the night also is thine: thou hast prepared the light and the sun."
—Psalm 74:16

The Distinguishing Traits of Christian Character

by Gardiner Spring
Recommended by: Bruce Bickel,
Pastor, Warrenville, Ill.

This masterfully written little volume caused me to lay my life alongside the objective standard of God's description of a true believer in order to "examine ourselves and prove ourselves whether we be in the faith" (2 Cor. 13:5).

Great confusion and subsequent delusion has flooded the professing church in our generation through a failure to distinguish the difference between two critical questions; what must one do to be saved? How may one know that he/she is saved? In most Evangelical circles today anyone who asks these questions is encouraged to simply rest on a text which declares that all believers are saved.

The answer given to these vital questions by Dr. Spring proceeds along a different line of evidence, one which has far more of the sanction of the Bible and of Historic Christianity.

Below is a quote concerning the confusion over good works.

"There is a wide difference between moral virtues and Christian graces. Christian graces spring from holy love and have their origin in holy motives. They regard chiefly the glory of God and the interests of the Kingdom and then govern the relationships of men with their fellowmen as God has required. The moral quality of actions lies in the disposition of the heart with which they are performed. A man may be very moral, but if the disposition of the heart with which the acts of morality are performed be not such as God requires and approves, though he may believe that he is going to Heaven, he is in the broad way to Hell."

How I Learned to Meditate

by Malcolm Smith
Recommended by: Melvin Bittenbender, P.E.,
Vice President, Macomber Associates, Inc.

Trying so hard to achieve things as a Civil Engineer, I made the "fullness of God in me" virtually a zero priority. Then I read that, through the grace of God, Christ died that, "we may be able to comprehend with all the saints what is the breadth and length and height and depth, and to know the love of Christ which surpasses knowledge, that you may be filled up to all the fullness of God." (Eph. 3:18-19)

"Christianity is the religion of *done*, all done by God. Every other religion is one of *doing*, seeking to attain God from man's end."

Now I remember the books that explained these Eastern philosophies. They all demanded discipline for self-improvement and control. The way of life I had come to in Jesus was simplicity itself. Jesus had said.

"Come to Me, all who are weary and heavy-laden, and I will give you rest. Take My yoke upon you, and learn from Me, for I am gentle and humble in heart; and you shall find rest for your souls. For My yoke is easy, and My load is light." (Matt. 11:28–30)

Entrance into this way began with a promise to do better, but a confession of total failure and then resting in Jesus the Lord. At that turning the new birth, the ultimate initiation, takes place.

"O sing unto the Lord a new song; for he hath done marvelous things."

—Psalm 98:1

Professional Football

Proverbs

by Solomon
Recommended by: Todd Blackledge,
Quarterback, Kansas City Chiefs

The book that I have profited from the most is without a doubt the Bible. In particular, I would encourage all aspiring, young leaders to read and meditate on the book of Proverbs. I believe two of the most important qualities of leadership are wisdom and humility. Proverbs ties these two qualities together perfectly.

"When pride comes, then comes dishonor, But with the humble is wisdom" (Proverbs 11:2).

Humility and the willingness to serve others – not only lead them – is the key to successful leadership.

Study of Romans

by Martyn Lloyd-Jones
Recommended by: Joe Shearin,
Football Player, Los Angeles Rams

The book that has had the most impact on my life is *Study of Romans.*

"In the same way count yourselves dead to sin but alive to God in Christ Jesus" (Romans 6:11).

Dr. Martyn Lloyd-Jones says, "To realize this takes away from us that old sense of hopelessness which we have all known and felt because of the terrible power of sin . . . How does it work? It works in this way: I lose my sense of hopelessness because I can say to myself that not only am I no longer under the dominion of sin, but I am under the dominion of another power that nothing can frustrate. However weak I may be, it is the power of God that is working in me."

Answers to Tough Questions

by Josh McDowell
Recommended by: Mike McLeod,
Green Bay Packers

The book consists of a series of common questions posed by skeptics of the Christian faith. Josh provides scriptural packed answers to each of the questions.

Ten Dates for Mates

by Dave and Claudia Arp
Recommended by: William Andrews,
Atlanta Falcons

This contains very useful information for married couples, and helps to increase communication and openness in a marriage.

Garden of Eden

by John Prest
Recommended by: Anthony Hancock,
Kansas City Chiefs

This is a very good book about the different scents of plants on earth, and the power of God.

The Mike MacIntosh Story:
For the Love of Mike

Recommended by: Debbie McPherson,
wife of Miles McPherson, San Diego Chargers

Mike MacIntosh is someone I know personally. I met him shortly before receiving his book. I became saved just before meeting Mike and had always looked at Christians as those who have always had a better grasp on life than most others. After meeting Mike and reading about his life, his struggle through childhood, his struggle with drugs and his trying so desperately to find the Lord, I realized then that I, too, could really be a Christian; and that I could become a child of God. I always thought I knew that anyone could be a Christian, but before meeting Mike and reading this book, there were periods of wondering about it.

For Better or for Best

by Gary Smalley
Recommended by: Jamie Woudenberg,
Pro Athletic Outreach

This book teaches women the how-tos of loving their husbands, and making them #1 in their lives.

"The *first step* in developing a genuine attitude of gratefulness is becoming aware that the benefits in your life have come from two main sources: other people and God. When confronted with this idea, one man said that it simply was not true. He started in business with nothing and had become extremely wealthy. He said, 'No one ever gave me anything.' He was asked how far he could have gone in business if he hadn't learned to read or write.

"If you stop to think about it, there are very few benefits in your life for which you can take sole credit."

Professional Football

Strengthening Your Grip

by Charles R. Swindoll
Recommended by: Carl Birdsong,
Football Player, St. Louis Cardinals

This book contains chapters on attitude and purity, as well as others which challenged me to improve my attitudes and walk with Christ. It enabled me to take a look at myself and realize areas that I needed to improve.

"Words can never adequately convey the incredible impact of our attitude toward life. The longer I live the more convinced I become that life is 10 percent what happens to us and 90 percent how we respond to it.

"This may shock you, but I believe the single most significant decision I can make on a day-to-day basis is my choice of attitude. It is more important than my past, my education, my bankroll, my successes or failures, fame or pain, what other people think of me or say about me, my circumstances, or my position. Attitude is that 'single string' that keeps me going or cripples my progress. It alone fuels my fire or assaults my hope. When my attitudes are right, there's no barrier too high, no valley too deep, no dream to extreme, no challenge too great for me."

I am the light of the world: he that followeth me shall not walk in darkness, but shall have the light of life.

—John 8:12

As a Man Thinketh

by James Allen
Recommended by: Glenn Bland,
President, Coaches Insurance Associates of America

I have chosen *As a Man Thinketh* by James Allen as the single book, other than the Bible, that has had the most profound effect on me during my lifetime.

The great wise men and philosophers of the past have disagreed about many things, but there is one thing about which they have been in complete and unanimous agreement: Homo sapiens is literally what he thinks, his character and station in life being the complete sum of all this thoughts. Emerson wrote, "A man is what he thinks about all day long." This very profound statement from one of mankind's most advanced thinkers serves also to express the opinions of his peers from ages past.

In *As a Man Thinketh*, James Allen addresses full well the mysteries of thought as it pertains to life while we are guests on planet earth. It was his chief aim "to stimulate men and women to the discovery and perception of the truth that:

"'They themselves are the makers of themselves,' by virtue of the thoughts which they choose and encourage; that mind is the master-weaver, both of the inner garment of character and the outer garment of circumstance, and that, as they may have hitherto woven in ignorance and pain they may now weave in enlightenment and happiness."

It is my belief that the golden key that unlocks the door to discovery of the abundant life is learning to cultivate and discipline the thought life. *As a Man Thinketh* can be an effective tool in helping one to achieve this end.

No great deed was ever wrought,
but what it first became a thought.

The Cross and the Switchblade

by Dave Wilkerson
Recommended by: Pat Boone,
Actor, Author, Recording Artist

When I picked up Dave Wilkerson's book, *The Cross and the Switchblade,* on a newsstand, I was on my way to Mexico City for a professional engagement. The juxtaposition of the two images intrigued me, and I decided to skim through the book.

It literally changed the direction of my life.

When I got to page 32 or 33, I had a severe attack of "goose-bumps"—because it was an account of a modern day miracle, and up till then I believed God would not perform miracles any longer. But this man was staking his life on the proposition that God was still in the miracle business, and would protect him and help him miraculously, every day!

It opened my eyes and spirit to a whole new dimension of life, and relationship with God, and I've never been the same. I also made the movie version, portraying David Wilkerson. That movie is being seen by tens of thousands of people every day in over 15 countries and languages, and has probably become the single most effective evangelistic instrument since the Bible itself. And Dave Wilkerson's story goes on!

I love them that love me; and those that seek me early shall find me.

—Proverbs 8:17

William Borden and Books

Missionary

Two books were his traveling companions at this time, and give some idea as to his talks in the colleges—one, the mission-study book for the year, Dr. Zwemer's *Unoccupied Mission Fields of Africa and Asia*, full of facts that were the strongest arguments, and the other a little paper-covered volume so worn and marked as to tell its own story. Many a journey it had taken with him, and its truths were being wrought into his deepest life. The little book, available through Back to the Bible, is *The Threefold Secret of the Holy Spirit*. Divided into three parts, it deals first with the secret of the incoming of the Holy Spirit; then with the secret of His fullness; and lastly with the secret of His constant manifestation in our lives. Borden's copy is marked in the way he had with all his best-loved books, one sentence standing out as meaning much to him: "The supreme human condition of the fulness of the Spirit is a life wholly surrendered to God to do His will."

—Mrs. Howard Taylor

"Works wrought in our own might are dead works; the chamber of prayer is the only true power-house; ministry, without anointing, is lifeless; we must touch Christ before we touch men; we can not pour out, if we have not received from Him. One touch of a live wire will thrill a man through and through, but you may touch him all day with a dead one and never quicken him. Faith without ministry is dead; ministry without faith—which is ministry *apart from Christ*—is declared by Christ Himself to be NOTHING."

Abundant Living

by E. Stanley Jones
Recommended by: Henry Brandt, Ph.D.,
Consulting Psychologist

This book helped me get my feet planted on solid rock when I was a new Christian.

Dr. Jones uses a variety of "ladders" to assist the reader. For example, one ladder has fifteen rungs which are enemies of human living. They are:

1. A lack of faith in something beyond oneself.
2. Self-Centeredness
3. Anger, resentments, hate
4. Fear, worry, anxiety
5. Unresolved guilt
6. Negativism and inferiority attitudes
7. Undisciplined desires
8. Insincerities, conscious and unconscious
9. Divided loyalties
10. Unbalanced virtues
11. Ignorance and lack of judgement
12. Bodily disharmony and disease
13. An unchristian social order
14. A lack of total discipline
15. A lack of creative, outgoing love.

Each rung contains Biblical guidance for putting the "How" into making corrections.

Still another ladder describes the marks of Jesus in our bodies. They are:

1. Forgiveness of injuries
2. No self pity
3. Joy-in spite of
4. Calm receptivity
5. Courage
6. The power to take it
7. Caring
8. Giving of oneself

This book got me started in searching for a Biblical basis for abundant living.

God's Best Secrets

by Andrew Murray
Recommended by: William R. Bright,
President, Campus Crusade for Christ International

Andrew Murray's book, *God's Best Secrets*, played a very important part in my life as a young Christian. Every day I was reminded of basic concepts of the Christian life that are essential if one is to truly experience the abundant, joyful, victorious, fruitful life which Jesus promised in John 10:10 and John 15:8. In his introduction, Andrew Murray says:

"The more I think of and pray about the state of religion in this country, and all over the world, the deeper my conviction becomes that the low state of the spiritual life of Christians is due to the fact that they do not realize that the aim and object of conversion is to bring the soul even here on earth, to a daily fellowship with the Father in heaven. When once this truth has been accepted, the believer will perceive how indispensable it is to the spiritual life of a Christian, to take time each day with God's Word and in prayer, to wait upon God for His presence and His love to be revealed.

"It has been my aim in writing this book to help Christians to see the absolute necessity of fellowship with the Lord Jesus. Without this the joy and power of God's Holy Spirit in daily life cannot be experienced. Many of God's children long for a better life, but do not realize the need of giving God time day by day in their inner chamber through His Spirit to renew and sanctify their lives."

As a new Christian, I was inspired day after day, and my standards of what a Christian should be, as I studied God's Word, were confirmed from the life and writings of the great saint of God.

Romans

by Apostle Paul
Recommended by: D. Stuart Briscoe,
Pastor, Milwaukee, Wisconsin

Without doubt, the most influential book in my life is the Bible. Unfortunately, I am not allowed to choose the Bible because it is technically 66 books so, presumably, to choose it would be to choose 65 more books than I am permitted! So I have chosen one of the 66 – *Romans*. Written by the Apostle Paul to a company of believers whom he had never met, the Epistle to the Romans is probably the greatest systematic presentation of the Christian gospel ever written.

It is profoundly serious in its explanation of who God is, what mankind has done and how God responded. It demonstrates the majesty of God's grace and the wonders of relationship with Him through faith.

But it is also profoundly practical. It shows mankind how to respond to God, how to appreciate what God offers, how to behave as a member of the believing community and even how to handle attitudes to family, business and government.

Whatever I can say about *Romans*, however, pales into insignificance when I remember that Augustine was converted to Christ through reading it, Luther was brought to a vital knowledge of salvation through it and John Wesley's assurance of peace with God was directly related to his understanding of it. Take those three men out of church history and you have some holes too big to fill. Imagine western history without those men and you'll find a very strange culture devoid of most of its value systems. Where would we all be without *Romans*?

The Richest Man in Babylon

by George S. Clason
Recommended by: W. Steven Brown, CPAE,
President, The Fortune Group

I recommend the book, *The Richest Man in Babylon*, by George S. Clason. It essentially teaches that as long as we spend all we earn, we are enslaved. In this circumstance we are forced to work because we have to, not because we want to. Financial pressure forces us to think of ourselves and interferes with our ability to concentrate on serving others.

In my twenty years of traveling throughout the free world working with sales managers and salespeople, I have observed a great deal of needless stress, frustration, and pressure.

Many times, men and women with talent, opportunity, and good incomes are unable to utilize their abilities and enjoy life because of their self-imposed financial pressures.

Mr. Clason outlines the proven disciplines necessary for us to manage our financial affairs successfully. In my opinion, the rampant lack of discipline in this area is the greatest deterrent to personal creativity and our ability to serve others.

"'Life is rich with many pleasures for men to enjoy.' Sharru Nada commented. 'Each has its place. I am glad that work is not reserved for slaves. Were that the case I would be deprived of my greatest pleasure. Many things do I enjoy but nothing takes the place of work.'"

Romans

by Donald Grey Barnhouse
Recommended by: Preacher Brown,
Pastor, Radio Bible Teacher, Baltimore, Md.

"Behold I am the Lord, the God of all flesh; is anything too hard for me? . . . Call to me and I will answer you and will tell you great and hidden things which you have not known" (Jer. 32:27; 33:3).

"Putting all of these thoughts together, we may arrive at the conclusions that to call upon the name of the Lord is to believe all that the name of the Lord stands for; to know the Lord in His qualities as Savior God, Lord of all; to approach Him through the altar of the cross; to recognize that there is no strength in ourselves but that all power dwells in Him, and to commit ourselves to Him in faith, desiring that He should act for us as He sees our need.

"We know both from the study of the Word and from our own lives that calling on the name of the Lord can be either a short experience or a long one. At times when we are in danger and trouble, our calling on the Lord is like the stabbing upthrust of a drowning man who clutches at that which can take him out of trouble. At other times when we are in sorrow and tribulation, our calling on the Lord is like the continual leaning of a wounded man who comes to rest upon a bed. Our calling on the Lord may well be the sudden thrust that turns into a constant trust."

Thy word have I hid in mine heart, that I might not sin against thee.
                                    —Psalm 119:11

Educators

David B. Burks, Dean
Harding University

There are many books which could be listed, but I am going to suggest *The Aroma of Christ*, by James S. Woodruff, published by G.T. Press. I am currently using it as a textbook for my class on business ethics. This text is important because it details the meaning on II Corinthians 2:14–16:1 and it is a very practical handbook on the development of ministry as it relates to all professionals.

The importance of this book is in helping students and others to understand the importance of their ministry as it deals, not only with what they do on Sunday but with what they do every day of their life, I am convinced that his point that all people are ministers is valid and needs to be accepted in the fullest sense of the word. The message of II Corinthians is, I believe, that all believers are ministers of the gospel and ambassadors for Christ and that this is something they must do in all of their life.

Martin E. Marty
Professor, University of Chicago

My faith has been shaped as much by the *Large Catechism* of Martin Luther as by any other book after the Bible. As a Lutheran, dedicated, fanatic, but also ecumenical and open-minded I have resorted constantly to this catechism and used it for instructing congregations. The proportion of space devoted to the Ten Commandments suggests that Luther was anything but antinomian or uninterested in care of the neighbor. The clues To God's continuing creation, the divine act of constantly bringing cosmos out of chaos, or the "gathered" and congregating character of faith prior to hearing and feeding on the Word, at the breast of the Church, has done its shaping. And, of course, so has its sacramental teaching.

Educators — Bible Teachers

Our Lord Prays for His Own

by Marcus Rainsford
Recommended by: John W. Cawood,
Chairman Biblical Studies,
Philadelphia College of the Bible

Yearly, I recommend to my students a reading of *Our Lord Prays for His Own*. I find a way to mention this book to all my students and frequently to those I speak to in churches.

Our Lord Prays for His Own is a study of the prayer given by Jesus as recorded in chapter 17 of the Gospel of John. The treatment Marcus Rainsford gives to these words is such that it makes one bow in awe to Christ. It is a rare book, worth reading more than once.

The Crises of the Christ

by G. Campbell Morgan
Recommended by: Wilbur M. Smith,
Author, Educator

In 1903, at the age of forty, appeared what is probably G. Campbell Morgan's greatest work, *The Crises of the Christ*. This had an enormous influence over me personally, in my younger ministry, and I would commend it to every minister of the Word as a volume to read, study, absorb, and repreach. This was followed by a companion work, *The Teaching of Christ*, ten years later.

Educators — Bible Teachers

Living Messages of the Books of the Bible

by G. Campbell Morgan
Recommended by: Dr. J. Vernon McGee,
Radio Bible Teacher, Author

Living Messages of the Books of the Bible, by G. Campbell Morgan, is a set of two volumes which introduced me to the whole Bible. Each book is filled with spiritual energy.

Strong's Concordance

by James Strong
Recommended by: Henry Morris,
President, Institute for Creations Research

It is exceedingly difficult to select any one book which has been the greatest help and influence in my life. Next to the Bible, I am sure that I have used *Strong's Concordance* more than any other book, and the insights gained from such detailed analysis of Biblical words have been a great help.

I think I would also suggest the very short but potent prose-poem, "Others May — You Cannot," written many years ago by George Watson.

Educators — Bible Teachers

Grace

by Dr. Lewis S. Chafer
Recommended by: Marvin J. Rosenthal,
International Director, Friends of Israel

I am rereading a book at this time which I have read at least six times in the last dozen years. It is simply called *Grace*, by the saintly late Dr. Lewis Sperry Chafer, founder of Dallas Theological Seminary.

In many of the Apostle Paul's epistles he wrote, "Grace be unto you, and peace, from God, our Father, and from the Lord Jesus Christ."

God's grace is the only basis for experiencing God's peace. This largely neglected but supremely important theme is masterfully dwelt with in the book, *Grace*.

The veneration we shall feel for the Bible as the depository of *saving knowledge* will be totally distinct, not only from what we attach to any other book, but from that admiration its other properties inspire; and the variety and antiquity of its history, the light it affords in various researches, its inimitable touches of nature, together with the sublimity and beauty so copiously poured over its pages, will be deemed subsidiary ornaments, the embellishments of the casket which contains the *pearl of great price*.

— Robert Hall

Educators—Bible Teachers

That You Might Believe

by Dr. Henry M. Morris
Recommended by: John C. Whitcomb,
Professor

As a young Christian student at Princeton University, recently returned from the war in Europe (1947), I was struggling with the authority of the Bible on the subject of ultimate origins. All I had been taught at Princeton was evolution. Could Genesis be literally true? In God's good providence, someone gave me a copy of Dr. Henry M. Morris, *That You Might Believe.* Here was a reputable engineer, and yet made an impressive, clear case for the literal interpretation of Genesis 1:11. The days of creation were 24-hour days. The world is not millions of years old. The Flood totally reshaped the earth's crust and laid down billions of fossils. In other words, the God of the Bible intended to be understood seriously, and evolution theories are in total error! God used this book and others like it to revolutionize my thinking on origins. Ten years later, Henry Morris and I co-authored *The Genesis Flood* which God has apparently used to help many people take the Bible at face value on the subject of original creation and the subsequent destruction of the world through water.

Every word of God is pure: he is a shield unto
them that put their trust in him.
—Proverbs 30:5

Educators

Here's How By Who's Who

by Grover Bell
Recommended by: A. Richart Bittle,
Christian School Administrator

Our lives are most assuredly affected by the books we read. Ironically, one that I have most recently enjoyed was a gift. *Here's How By Who's Who.* I've been enjoying that book during "brown bag" lunch hours I spend at my desk. The book's format permits short, enjoyable reading moments. Brief biographies and inspirational messages from successful men afford marvelous daily lessons that I am able to apply to my own life.

One short message that really touched my heart was penned by one of my boyhood idols – Bob Feller, of Baseball's Hall of Fame. Bob admonishes a young man to "budget his time religiously, because wasting time is just as serious as breaking any of the Ten Commandments. The Lord allotted us a certain amount of time on earth and wasting it is being ungrateful and selfish, not only to the God above, but to our fellow citizens."

"Blessed is he that readeth." – Revelation 1:3

Knowing God

by J. I. Packer
Recommended by: Dr. David L. Burnham,
Pastor, Boca Raton, Florida

A book that has been a great influence on me was *Knowing God*, by J. I. Packer. It aided in the development of my concept of God.

I believe the author was able to take thoughts that I had had in a variety of forms, but with clarity and direction, state them in a way that really anchored my own concept of God. And I believe that your concept of God determines your concept of yourself.

"This is momentous knowledge. There is unspeakable comfort – the sort of comfort that energises, be it said, not enervates – in knowing that God is constantly taking knowledge of me in love, and watching over me for my good. There is tremendous relief in knowing that His love to me is utterly realistic, based at every point on prior knowledge of the worst about me, so that no discovery now can disillusion Him about me, in the way I am so often disillusioned about myself, and quench His determination to bless me. There is, certainly, great cause for humility in the thought that He sees all the twisted things about me that my fellow-men do not see (and am I glad!), and that He sees more corruption in me than that which I see in myself (which, in all conscience, is enough). There is however, equally great incentive to worship and love God in the thought that, for some unfathomable reason, He wants me as His friend, and desires to be my friend, and has given His Son to die for me in order to realise this purpose. We cannot work these thoughts out here, but merely to mention them is enough to show how much it means to know, not merely that we know God, but that He knows us."

Great Missionaries and Books

William Carey

When at twenty years of age, Carey was slowly piecing together "the doctrines of the Word of God" into something like a system which would at once satisfy his own spiritual and intellectual needs, and help him to preach to others, a little volume was published, of which he wrote: – "I do not remember even to have read any book with such raptures." It was *Help to Zion's Travellers: being an attempt to remove various Stumbling-Blocks out of the Way, relating to Doctrinal, Experimental, and Practical Religion*, by Robert Hall. The writer was the father of the greater Robert Hall, a venerable man, who, in his village church of Arnsby near Leicester, had already taught Carey how to preach. The book is described as an "attempt to relieve discouraged Christians" in a day of gloominess and perplexity, that they might devote themselves to Christ through life as well as be found in Him in death. Carey made a careful synopsis of it in an exquisitely neat hand on the margin of each page. The worm-eaten copy, which he treasured even in India, is now deposited in Bristol College.

David Livingstone

David Livingstone at ten years of age was put into a cotton factory near Glasgow. Out of his first week's wages he bought a Latin Grammar, and studied in the night schools for years. He would sit up and study until midnight unless his mother drove him to bed, notwithstanding he had to be at the factory at six in the morning. He mastered Virgil and Horace in this way, and read extensively, besides studying botany. So eager and thirsty for knowledge was he, that he would place this book before him on the spinning-jenny, and amid the deafening roar of machinery would pore over its pages.

Tough Times Never Last, But Tough People Do

by Robert H. Schuller
Recommended by: Dr. Paul Yonggi Cho,
Pastor, Seoul, Korea

One of the many books which has blessed me is entitled, *Tough Times Never Last, But Tough People Do,* by Dr. Robert H. Schuller.

Two short paragraphs I would like to submit from the book as being very appropriate are as follow:

"Every spiritual leader in the world today has felt the pressures and demands of leadership that often converge suddenly in the form of crisis situations, all at one time and all clamoring for first priority attention. The greater the area of responsibility, the more tough times there are until it would seem that they are more than one person can handle; however, I have learned that tough times do not last forever. They teach us to be tough for God and learn to depend more on Him, and in learning to depend more on Him, our capacity has been enlarged to do more for God."

"'If God is for us, who can be against us?' (Rom. 8:31) That is the ultimate secret of becoming tough enough to face the toughest battle and win! Only then can you be sure that your life will prove the truth of the title of this book: *Tough Times Never Last, But Tough People Do!* – eternally!"

Jewels from the Queen of the Dark Chamber

by Christiana Tsai
Recommended by: Moses C. Chow,
President, Ambassadors for Christ, Inc.

The book I would like to recommend is *Jewels from the Queen of the Dark Chamber*. I had met with the author, Christiana Tsai, daily for the last three years. On August 25, 1984, Miss Tsai was promoted to glory.

Herbert Griffin, Director for North America, China Island Mission, said:

"The very name Christiana reminds us of the pilgrim in Bunyan's immortal allegory. More than that, the life story of Christiana Tsai depicts the unusual experiences in the pilgrim pathway of a Chinese believer. The facts presented in this autobiography are truly stranger than fiction. How marvelous that in early girlhood Christiana, though the daughter of a wealthy Confucian official, should meet the Lord and respond to His claim! Her mind and heart were early impressed with the divine declaration, 'I am the way, the truth, and the life.' Not only did Christiana appropriate this truth for herself, but she devoted her life to the making known to the One whom she recognized as Saviour of the world and the hope of her nation. Thus Christiana became a pilgrim of The Splendid Way."

In this was manifest the Love of God toward us, because that God sent His only begotten Son into the World, that we might live through Him. We love Him because He first loved us.
—1 John 4:9,19

With Christ in the School of Prayer

by Andrew Murray
Recommended by: Evelyn Christenson,
Author, Conference Speaker

Andrew Murray's *With Christ in the School of Prayer* has produced more personal commitments to God than any other book about prayer I have read. His chapters are short and demand so much personal attention that I never can read more than one chapter at a time. I have to let its message burrow deep into my heart and then work its way into my life through prayer.

I read Murray's book after teaching prayer for almost ten years and writing a book on the subject. But by the end of chapter one, I felt the necessity to pray all over again this prayer with him:

"Lord Jesus! I ask Thee this day to enroll my name among those who confess that they know not how to pray as they ought, and specially ask Thee for a course of teaching in prayer. Lord! teach me to tarry with Thee in the school, and give Thee time to train me. May a deep sense of my ignorance, of the wonderful privilege and power of prayer, the need of the Holy Spirit as the Spirit of prayer, lead me to cast away my thoughts of what I think I know, and make me kneel before Thee in the true teachableness and poverty of spirit."

And I voluntarily enrolled again in Christ's school of prayer – with this book as my guide.

In one chapter Murray writes about faith, using as his text Mark 11:24. Here he explains that "before we can believe, we must discover and know what God's will is; believing is the exercise of a soul surrendered and given up to the influence of the Word and the Spirit; but when once we do believe nothing shall be impossible."

St. Francis of Assisi

by Johannes Joergensen
Recommended by: Douglas Coe,
Director, International Christian Leadership

The book that has meant so much to me is called *St. Francis of Assisi*. It is a translation by Johannes Joergensen. This book has helped to clarify for me one of the fundamental secrets of the lives of men and women who are used of God. The main focus in the life of St. Francis and others who have found this secret is not the evangelization of other people. The secret is reaching a preoccupation with Jesus Christ, that is, to love God with my own heart and not the preaching to others. If I want to reach the whole world, I need to first reach myself for Christ. A quotation that I would like to share with you is found on page 198 of this book.

. . . "There is a great difference," said he (Brother Giles), "between a sheep which bleats and one which grazes. For braying does no one any good, but grazing does itself good. It is so with a Friar Minor who preaches, and one who prays and works. A thousand and again a thousand times better is it to teach oneself than to teach the whole world."

Another time he broke out thus: "Who is richer – he who has only a little garden and cultivates it, or he to whom the whole world was given and who does nothing with it? So much wisdom does not help to salvation, but he who really wishes to know much must work much and bow his head low."

This book on the life of St. Francis is another way of saying that God's ways are not our ways as proclaimed in Isaiah 55. The way to reach the whole world is not by greater and greater preaching but is more an effort of the heart to let Jesus Christ be to the individual person all that Christ wants to be.

Pensees

by Blaise Pascal
Recommended by: Dr. Robert Coleman,
Professor, Trinity Seminary

I think that for me the classical *Pensees* by Blaise Pascal would stand tall on any list. Ranging from a few cryptic words to short essays, this collection of "thoughts" by the devout French scientist, written about 1660, is one of literature's most profound insights to human experience from the perspective of Christian commitment.

God's saving Revelation, comes only through divine illumination in the believer's soul. "It is the heart which experiences God, and not the reason. This, then, is faith. God felt by the heart" (Pensees, Article 278). By this Pascal does not mean mystical emotion, but rather, an intuitive love for God Himself. Those awakened by grace will have this perception. Moreover, God has so constructed the universe that He will be found of those who search for Him will all their heart.

The focus is Jesus Christ, the object of all Scripture, for He alone incarnated the Infinite Word in our human estate. In His Person is revealed both the truth of God and the truth of humanity. Yet only persons who renounce self-love will know what this means. Herein is exposed the error of those who do not find the Truth. A genuine Christian does not squabble over signs; he or she humble bows in adoration before the Sovereign Lord of all.

It is the reverence before the crucified, risen and glorified Messiah-Savior, which speaks to my soul. And, with Pascal, seeing the emptiness of human achievement, I want to expend my remaining energies to know Him in Whom alone are hidden all the wisdom and the glory of God.

Spirit-Controlled Temperament

by Tim LaHaye
Recommended by: William H. Cook,
Pastor, Author, Bartellsville, Oklahoma

Tim LaHaye's *Spirit-Controlled Temperament* is a book that kept me glued to the pages. Tim eases us into finding our temperament (sanguine, choleric, phlegmatic, or melancholy) and then has us laughing at our own weaknesses. He is an expert at identifying the strengths and weaknesses of the various temperaments and putting us in a working mood about how to improve.

Here's a choice comment about "grasshopper vision."

"If we really believe God is able to supply all our needs, it is going to cause us to have peace and joy and will eliminate doubt, fear, and striving. Many of God's people, like the nation of Israel, waste 40 years out in the desert of life because they do not believe God. Far too many Christians have 'grasshopper vision.' They are like the ten faithless spies who saw the giants in the land of Canaan and came home to cry, 'We are as grasshoppers in their sight.' How could they possibly know what the giants thought of them? You can be sure they did not get close enough to ask! They did just what we often do—jumped to a faithless conclusion."

Psychological Letdown

"There is a natural psychological letdown whenever a great project has been completed. A very energetic and creative individual can be happy and contended while working toward a long-range goal. But when the goal is reached, it is often followed by a period of depression because the individual has not been able to mount another project to succeed the one he has concluded." (Tim then reminds us depression is eliminated when new projects and higher goals are set to replace those already completed.)

The Life that Wins

by Charles Trumbull
Recommended by: Harold Coulter,
former Los Angeles Teacher and School Principal

I'm 84 years old now. Many years ago when I was reading *The Life that Wins*, by the great Presbyterian preacher named Trumbull, I came to the words in italics which stated that "the life that wins" is just Jesus Christ. This came as a heavenly revelation. It turned me around and showed me that Jesus Christ lives in me and wants to do all His work in and through me. I am to be His vessel and His mouthpiece:

"Jesus Christ does not want to be our helper; He wants to be our life. He does not want us to work for Him. He wants us to let Him do His work through us, using us as we use a pencil to write with—better still, using us as one of the fingers on his hand."

"And remember that Christ Himself is better than any of His blessings; better than the power, or the victory, or the service, that He grants. Christ creates spiritual power; but Christ is better than power. He is God's best; He is God; and we may have this best: we may have Christ, yielding to Him in such completeness and abandonment of self that it is no longer we that live, but Christ liveth in us. Will you thus take Him?"

I also highly recommend *Don't Waste Your Sorrows*, by Paul Billheimer. It is a paperback book that should be read by every Christian who has physical and other kinds of problems.

Morning & Evening

by Charles Haddon Spurgeon
Recommended by: W. A. Criswell,
Author, Pastor, Dallas, Texas

A special book in my ministry is Spurgeon's *Morning & Evening.*

"If there be not time to read both our morning portion and the usual chapter, we earnestly entreat that our book may be dispensed with, for it were a sore affliction to us to know that any family read the Word of God less on our account. We have it in our heart to lead our friends to search their Bibles more than ever, and therefore we have culled passages of corners and nooks of Scripture, that curiosity might lead to a search for their context; we shall be disappointed indeed, if, after all, we frustrate our own design by diverting one moment of time to the perusal of our remarks which ought to have been given to searching the Word of God itself."

"'Grow in grace, and in the knowledge of our Lord and Saviour Jesus Christ.'—2 Peter iii. 18.

"Grow in grace—not in one grace only, but in *all* grace. Grow in that root-grace, *faith.* Believe the promises more firmly than you have done. Let faith increase in fulness, constancy, simplicity. Grow also in *love.* Ask that your love may become extended, more intense, more practical, influencing every thought, word, and deed. Grow likewise in *humility.* Seek to lie very low, and know more of your own nothingness. As you grow *downward* in humility, seek also to grow *upward*—having nearer approaches to God in prayer and more intimate fellowship with Jesus. May God the Holy Spirit enable you to *'grow in the knowledge of our Lord and Saviour.'* He who grows not in the knowledge of Jesus, refuses to be blessed."

Success, Motivation, and the Scriptures

by Dr. William Cook
Recommended by: William Van Crouch,
Professional Speaker, Insurance Executive

This book helped me understand that the believer is a winner; that the great dividing line of the Bible is John 10:10. "The thief cometh not, but for to steal, and to kill, and to destroy; I am come (Jesus) that they have life, and that they might have it more abundantly."

Is God interested in your success? There are many opinions today. Do I set goals or "take no thought for the morrow?" One author says, have a self controlled life; another says, I need a Christ controlled life. Do I take care of number one and at the very same time "humble myself in the sight of God?" The frustration can really grow.

Our adversary, the devil, would attempt to divide us by having us believe that a desire to succeed is an enemy of humility. That God is anti-personal motivation; and that a positive attitude is an enemy to a total commitment to Christ.

When the believer decides for himself that God meant what he said, and said what He meant, takes a stand on and begins to do the uncompromised word of God, big things begin to happen. This book tells the believer how to get the power of God going in their behalf. *Success, Motivation, and the Scriptures* helps a person set godly priorities in three key areas; the spiritual area, motivation area, and success area. This book also shows the unsaved person his necessity for God and His participation in their individual success.

This book helped me to understand that all the motivation a person will ever need or could possibly utilize is found in the person of the Lord Jesus Christ.

The Mark of a Christian

by Francis A. Schaeffer
Recommended by: Mary Crowley,
CEO, Home Interiors and Gifts, Inc.

The Bible has had the greatest influence on my life, for I grew up before the days of television when we had the privilege of reading and thinking and talking.

There are two other books that have had a tremendous influence on my thinking. One is small. One is medium sized. The small one is written by Charles E. Hummel. The other book is *The Mark of a Christian*, written by Dr. Francis Schaeffer. Here is a summary of the last paragraph, found on page 204. "Love – in the unity it attests to – is the mark Christ gave Christians to wear before the world. Only with this mark may the world know that Christians are indeed Christians, and that Jesus was sent by the Father."

"'Little children, yet a little while I am with you. Ye shall seek me; and as I said unto the Jews, whither I go, ye cannot come; so now I say to you. A new commandment I give unto you, That ye love one another; as I have loved you, that ye also love one another. By this shall all men know that ye are my disciples, if ye have love one to another.' (John 13:33–35) This passage reveals the mark that Jesus gives to label a Christian not just in one era or in one locality but at all times and all places until Jesus returns."

"Teach me thy way, O Lord." – *Psalm 86:1*

The Weight of Glory

by C. S. Lewis
Recommended by: James A. Davey,
Pastor, Seattle, Washington

C. S. Lewis has had an impact on my life. Trying to determine the most important book or thought I have gleaned from him is a little bit like deciding between mint and chocolate ice cream. On any given day you might like one or the other. Here is an excerpt from his essay *The Inner Ring*. Taken from the small volume of essays entitled *The Weight of Glory*, it was recently a factor in a major career decision.

"The quest of the Inner Ring will break your hearts unless you break it. But if you break it, a surprising result will follow. If in your working hours you make the work your end, you will presently find yourself all unawares inside the only circle in your profession that really matters. You will be one of the sound craftsmen, and other sound craftsmen will know it. This group of craftsmen will by no means coincide with the Inner Ring or the Important People or the People in the Know. It will not shape that professional policy or work up that professional influence which fights for the professional as a whole against the public: nor will it lead to those periodic scandals and crises which the Inner Ring produces. But it will do those things which that profession exists to do and will in the long run be responsible for all the respect which that profession in fact enjoys and which the speeches and advertisements cannot maintain."

Twenty Centuries of Great Preaching

edited by
Clyde Faut and William Pinson
Recommended by: James E. Davey,
Pastor

Just a year before the appearance of this set, a book from the publisher declared that great preaching is no longer a worthy ministerial goal. I suspect that this monumental set will be a useful tool in preachers' libraries long after the former book is forgotten. Since the high purchase price would seem to augur limited sales and little profit for Word, the set can perhaps be viewed as a form of penance.

A brief summary of major events and dates in the lives of each of the ninety-six preachers sampled is preceded by a portrait of the preacher that often demolishes the myth of physical charisma. This generally well-written but necessarily taut biography reveals shaping influences on the preacher and pays particular attention to his method of sermon preparation and delivery. A bibliography concludes each introduction. Each volume has a fold-out fly-leaf relating the lifetime of each preacher to the social, political, economic, and religious events of this day.

If one wishes to sharpen his pulpit abilities by reading at least one sermon for each one he produces, he could well begin with the 413 samples in these volumes.

Move Ahead with Possibility Thinking

by Robert Schuller
Recommended by: Guy Davidson,
Pastor, Tempe, Arizona

Move Ahead with Possibility Thinking has been the greatest motivational book for me. Even though I cannot go along with all its principles, it is the one that motivated me to begin my church in 1966 and open its doors in 1967. So I'm indebted for the ideas that motivated me. The thought that stood out most of all was simply this: "Find a need and fill it."

"The possibility thinkers resemble the hummingbird that looks for and finds honey, often in the most unlikely and unthinkable places. The possibility thinkers perceptively probe every problem, proposal, and opportunity to discover the positive aspects present in almost every human situation.

"They are people – just like you – who when faced with a mountain do not quit. They keep on striving until they climb over, find a pass through, tunnel underneath – or simply stay and turn their mountain into a gold mine."

The greatest book spiritually for my life has been *The Pulpit Commentary.* I find its volumes very helpful in giving, not only background, but insight and food for my own soul.

Failure: The Back Door to Success

by Erwin W. Lutzer
Recommended by: Carl Dixon,
Investment Executive

This book puts failure and success into the perspective of a Christ-centered life. As a businessman, I desire to be Christ-centered, not just Christianized. The book states that successful people are those who apply God's remedy for failure.

The opening story confronts us with a sincere, committed Christian. He does everything he is supposed to do, but has everything turn out wrong, ending in the ultimate failure . . . suicide! What a contrast from the multitude of books that falsely tell us that Christians are always healthy and successful. Lutzer masterfully explains why it is wrong to compare ourselves to other people or worldly standards. He then explains how to allow God to empower us to live a dynamic life, less and less affected by circumstances. Lutzer teaches about forgiveness, self-acceptance, discouragement and tragedy, leaving the reader with great hope.

Listen to a paragraph near the end of the book.

"Better to love God and die unknown than to love the world and be a hero; better to be content with poverty than to die a slave to wealth; better to have taken some risks and lost than to have done nothing and succeeded at it; better to have lost some battles than to have retreated from the war; better to have failed when serving God than to have succeeded when serving the devil. What a tragedy to climb the ladder of success only to discover that the ladder was leaning against the wrong wall!"

Don't read this book unless you are tired of the multitude of self-help platitudes that only patch up the outer man, leaving the inner man totally lost.

A History of the English Speaking Peoples

by Winston Churchill
Recommended by: James C. Dobson, Ph.D.,
President, Focus on the Family

My favorite books are published under the title, *A History of the English Speaking Peoples*, by Winston Churchill. This series is a marvelous, four-volume overview of English history from the time of Christ to World War II. Though not a "Christian text," there are innumerable Biblical truths evident in its description of the surge of human history and conflict. Most importantly, I saw in this 2000 year account the utter folly of human pride, lust, greed and power. Like Solomon, it leads me to conclude, "Vanity of vanities, all is vanity." (Eccl. 1:2)

"George Washington holds one of the proudest titles that history can bestow. He was the Father of his Nation. Almost alone his staunchness in the War of Independence held the American colonies to their united purpose. His services after victory had been won were no less great. His firmness and example while first President restrained the violence of faction and postponed a national schism for sixty years. . . . He filled his office with dignity and inspired his administration with much of his own wisdom."

"The Constitution was a reaffirmation of faith in the principles painfully evolved over the centuries by the English-speaking peoples. It enshrined long-standing English ideas of justice and liberty, henceforth to be regarded on the other side of the Atlantic as basically American. In its fundamental doctrine the American people acquired an institution which was to command the same respect and loyalty as in England are given to Parliament and Crown."

Life Is Tremendous

by Charles "T" Jones
Recommended by: S. J. Domenick,
President, Federal Credit Union

Without exception, this book has greatly changed my attitudes as a leader, helping me to learn how to better live my life. I was so impressed that I ordered 50 copies for distribution to my counterparts in 40 states and our corporation board of directors. All it takes is to practice the "7 Laws of Leadership" which are so aptly recorded in the book. The section "3 Decisions of Life" gives great guidelines for a successful life regardless of the profession you are involved in. The quote, "Life's greatest challenge is not being a man's man but God's man," is one I keep remembering, and it is also aptly stated that, "Leaders are Readers"—this phrase has been proven over and over where you find success in people at the top. In all of the writings documented by mankind, these great words of wisdom are unsurpassed:

"The Greatest thought is God"
"The Greatest thing is love"
"The Greatest mystery is death"
"The Greatest challenge is life"
"The Greatest waste of time is hate and the most expensive indulgence is pride."

If we could overcome these, then we should all be closer to our maker.

The Pursuit of God

by A. W. Tozer
Recommended by: Stephen Duff,
Pastor, Baltimore, Maryland

A. W. Tozer is boldly honest in *The Pursuit of God*. It's not hard to find Bible teachers today, but it is extremely rare to find a man of God whose life is Christ 24 hours a day. If someone gives himself unreservedly and fervently to the pursuit of God, to the furtherance of the Kingdom of God in any creative way possible, and makes a local church with a worldwide vision his lifestyle with dogmatism and intense desire, most of evangelical Christianity would consider him to be fanatical and unbalanced.

This is not for lukewarm Christians. It is strictly red-hot with desire for continual and ever-increasing experiential fellowship with, and motivation by, God.

I have read *The Pursuit of God* at least seven times. If you want a book that will encourage your capacity for the Living God, I give it my highest recommendation. No one has regretted saturating his soul with its depths.

Let me present you a few quotes to give the tenor of the book.

". . . we Christians are in real danger of losing God amid the wonders of His Word. We have almost forgotten that God is a Person and, as such, can be cultivated as any person can."

"To have found God and still to pursue Him is the soul's paradox of love, scorned indeed by the too-easily-satisfied religionist, but justified in happy experience by the children of the burning heart."

"The blessed ones who possess the Kingdom are they who have repudiated every external thing and have rooted from their hearts all sense of possessing."

Enjoy this book and light your candle at its flame!

The Bishop of Wall Street

by Sara C. Palmer
Recommended by: H. Creighton Dunlap,
Director, St. Paul's House

Roger Babson, the statistician wrote that, whenever he felt a little discouraged, he would pick up and read a little excerpt from "Dad Hall – Bishop of Wall Street". Many have said they couldn't put this book down.

Dad Hall was even closer to me than a father. Through him I found new life in Christ – became a converted Episcopal Vestryman and received God's call to the ministry. At the age of 75 he held Lenten Mission Week in our Episcopal Church in Philadelphia. Although a Vestryman, I had no intention of attending these services, feeling I was too busy making appraisals for Trust Companies, etc. But, when I looked out the window of our Real Estate office, one evening, I saw him preaching on the lawn of our church. I said to my brother and partner Alex, "If he has the conviction to preach out-of-doors, I am going over to hear him!" I never saw or heard of a minister preaching in the open-air before, especially an Episcopal minister.

In the same year he brought me to the Saviour he had had a stroke as he preached in an open-air meeting, and his left side was paralyzed. Through prayer and chiropracty he was recovering from this, when the telephone rang; the caller said, "Sorry wrong number." Dad Hall said, "It's the right number for Heaven" and gave him a Bible verse and message. The caller passes this on, and since then we've had 1,850,000 calls – some lives have been saved from suicide and many souls saved for eternity.

When he came to New York City he preached in Times Square and Wall Street, and became known as "The Bishop of Wall Street." In seven years of noonday preaching, seven men went into the ministry.

The Great Evangelical Disaster

by Francis A. Schaeffer
Recommended by: Bruce Dunn,
Pastor, Peoria, Illinois

This book brought home to me the urgency of our times. Dr. Schaeffer shows why the word "evangelical" has become meaningless. There is almost nothing they will stand for or against. Clearly, time is running out.

"If we look again at the command in John 13, we will notice some important things. First of all, this is a command to have a special love to all true Christians, all born-again Christians. From the scriptural viewpoint, not all who call themselves Christians are Christians, and that is especially true in our generation. The meaning of the word *Christian* has been reduced to practically nothing. Surely, there is no word that has been so devalued unless it is the word *God* itself. Central to semantics is the idea that a word as a symbol has no meaning until content is put into it. This is quite correct. Because the word *Christian* as a symbol has been made to mean so little, it has come to mean everything and nothing.

"But we must be careful of the opposite error. We must include everyone who stands in the historic-biblical faith whether or not he is a member of our own party or our own group.

"But even if a man is not among the true Christians, we still have the responsibility to love him as our neighbor. So we cannot say, 'Now here's somebody that, as far as I can tell, does not stand among the group of true Christians, and therefore I don't have to think of him any more; I can just slough him off.' Not at all. He is covered by the second commandment."

Pilgrim's Progress

by John Bunyan
Recommended by: David duPlessis,
Pastor

I was the first in a South African family of nine boys, and thus was expected to be a perfect example to my brothers. That is one reason why the Bible was the first book to make an impact upon my childhood days. Devotions every morning and evening were the strict rule of life, and so before I was twelve years old, I had read the Bible through around the table.

At age twelve, I had a profound encounter with Jesus as my Savior. From then on, I wanted to be like Him. His earthly father, like mine, was a carpenter. But mine was also a reader, and in his bookshelf I soon found *Pilgrim's Progress*. Here in simple story language were the truths of the Bible. They rooted my life more firmly in the Word of God.

In later years, when more and more problems appeared, I found Bunyan's *Holy War* a great help. His writings so impressed me that I often wondered whether one would have to go to prison in order to write such wonderful books.

I thank God for books, both classic and modern. But as the apostle John reminds us at the end of his gospel, there are yet other things that Jesus did (and is doing) that, if they were published, the world itself would not be large enough to contain.

Freedom of Simplicity

by Richard J. Foster
Recommended by: Ralph Eaton,
President, Eaton Investments, Inc.

A book that I have thoroughly enjoyed reading is *Freedom of Simplicity*. There is so much in it that is applicable to my own life that I am earnestly striving to achieve Mr. Foster's simple and practical, yet profound, suggestion for simplicity in my own lifestyle.

In the very first chapter, we are told that Christian simplicity can free us from the modern mania of fast-paced living that leaves us feeling fractured and fragmented, strained and hurried, and with a breathlessness that threatens to overwhelm us. Simplicity in living allows us to see material things for what they are – goods to enhance life, not to oppress life. Simplicity enables us to live lives of integrity in the face of the terrible realities of present day living.

In its two hundred pages, *Freedom of Simplicity* touches on the Biblical Foundation for simplicity and the Practice of Simplicity in personal, family, social and church life.

It is a down-to-earth treatise on living a simple, godly, Christian life. I shall never be the same.

> *. . . Man shall not live by bread alone, but by every word that proceedeth out of the mouth of God.*
>
> *—Matthew 4:4*

Bruchko

by Bruce E. Olson
Recommended by: Jon Edwards,
Pastor, Colorado Springs, Colorado

I believe one of the supreme examples of the triumph of powerlessness is the story of Bruce Olson, a pioneer missionary in the twentieth century. *Bruchko* is a spellbinder, a story of a nineteen-year-old college dropout who walked into the Colombian rain forest and took the Gospel of Christ and modern medicine and hygiene to a stoneage tribe known as the Motilones. Previous contacts by white men had been limited to oil company workers who ventured into the territory and were promptly murdered by the Indians.

But Bruce Olson walked into Motilone territory alone, compelled by a deep conviction that God wanted him to take the Gospel to those people. Having been turned down by a mission board as too young and untrained he went with almost no money, church support or help from his parents. His training consisted of a flair for linguistics and a couple years of language study.

Accepted by the Motilones, Bruce adapted to their lifestyle, learned their tonal language and adapted the message of Jesus Christ to their culture in a way they could understand. Hundreds came to Christ, and whole villages were transformed. Bruce put their language into writing, and has translated several New Testament books into the Motilone language. He has taught the Indians health measures, agricultural techniques and the value of preserving their cultural heritage.

It is the story of a young man who really believed God and who followed Christ in a simple, straightforward way. Here, truly, is an example of II Corinthians 12:9 "My grace is sufficient for you, for my power is perfected in weakness."

If Only He Knew

by Gary Smalley
Recommended by: Norm Evans, Former Captain, Miami
Dolphins, President, Professional Christian Athletes

My favorite is Gary Smalley's, *If Only He Knew*. This book really shook me up because I thought I truly loved my wife and was doing a fairly good job of meeting her needs. *If Only He Knew* showed me how far off base I was when I came to knowing, understanding and truly loving my wife in a way that she needed. It has revolutionized our marriage.

If Only He Knew is a book for husbands who genuinely desire a rich and lasting marriage relationship, but aren't quite sure where to begin. The recent barrage of how-to books has taught men how-to-make-it-in-business, how-to-get-rich, and even how-to-dress-for-success. Yet one of the most basic and important how-tos of life has been ignored: how to be a good husband.

If Only He Knew teaches a husband how to build a marriage that will last as long as it was originally meant to last. It teaches a husband how to do this in three ways: by giving the ten basic steps needed to strengthen a marriage; by explaining the deepest needs a woman has; and by showing him how to meet those needs.

But thanks be to God, which giveth us the victory through our Lord Jesus Christ. Therefore, my beloved brethren, be ye stedfast, unmoveable, always abounding in the work of the Lord, forasmuch as ye know that your labour is not in vain in the Lord.
—I Corinthians 15:57,58

Interdenominational Ministries

The Training of the Twelve

by A. B. Bruce
Recommended by: Ted W. Engstrom,
President, World Vision International

The Training of the Twelve by A. B. Bruce is one of the most helpful books on leadership that I've come across. It has to do with Christ investing Himself in His disciples; teaching them to practice daily disciplines that foster spiritual growth and leadership. For instance, He made frequent efforts to instill the practice of prayer into His disciples. In the Sermon on the Mount, He cautioned His hearers about pharisaic showiness and heathenish repetition, and presented prayer as a model of simplicity, comprehensiveness, and brevity. In another section, the book outlines what could only be called "the rewards of self-sacrifice." The contrast between what is forsaken and what rewards are received is striking. The twelve had forsaken fishing boats and nets, and they were to be rewarded with thrones; and everyone who forsakes anything for the kingdom of God is promised a return of a hundred-fold. Bruce has given us a tremendous lesson on the generosity of the Master whom Christians serve.

The Holy Spirit in Today's World

by David Hubbard
Recommended by: Ira "Doc" Eshelman
President, Sports World Ministries

Interdenominational Misistries

The Pursuit of God

by A. W. Tozer
Recommended by: George Sanchez,
Director, International Ministries, The Navigators

"We pursue God because, and only because, He has first put an urge within us that spurs us to the pursuit. "No man can come to me," said our Lord, "except the Father which hath sent me draw him," and it is by this very prevenient *drawing* that God takes from us every vestige of credit for the act of coming. The impulse to pursue God originates with God, but the outworking of impulse is our following hard after Him; and all the time we are pursuing Him we are already in His hand: "Thy right hand upholdeth me."

The Shepherd Psalm

by F. B. Meyer
Recommended by: Jack McCalister
Founder of World Literature Crusade

I have loved many books but this is the most inspired book ever written outside of Holy Scripture.
"We pass through many a valley of shadow ere we reach THE *valley.* And whenever we feel our souls overcast, we should stay to consider if there be a cause arising from our neglect or sin. If there be, a moment's confession will bring us out again into the light. But if there be none, so far as we can tell, then let us be brave to plod on. Every step has been measured out for us, even as it has been trodden before us. And God is testing us, to see whether we can trust Him in the dark as well as in the light; and whether we can be as true to Him when all pleasurable emotions have faded off our hearts, as when we walked with Him in the light."

The Normal Christian Life

by Watchman Nee
Recommended by: Dr. Jerry Falwell,
Pastor, Educator, Author
Lynchburg, Virginia

Shortly after God led me to establish the Thomas Road Baptist Church in Lynchburg, Virginia, in June, 1965, someone gave me a copy of *The Normal Christian Life*. At that time, I was searching for a deeper understanding of what the Christian life is all about. I can sincerely say this book has been used of God more effectively in my life than any book outside the Bible itself. Watchman Nee has put into words the true simplicity of the victorious Christian life. His emphasis is "Christ in you."

Every new convert ought to read this book immediately after his conversion. If I had known of this book after my conversion in 1952, I could have avoided wasting many, many years struggling to please God through Christian service. Down through the years, I have distributed hundreds of copies of this book to my friends. The best description of this book is "revelation." There is no question in my mind that God has given to Watchman Nee special wisdom in defining the dynamic of the Christian life as no other man has. You will probably read this book several times. Each time, the Holy Spirit will make the indwelling of Christ a more blessed reality to you.

I am the way, the truth, and the life: no man cometh unto the Father, but by me.

—John 14:6

The Lord of the Rings

by J. R. Tolkien
Recommended by: Dale Ferrier
Certified Professional Speaker

J. R. R. Tolkien's epic trilogy is one of those stories that sneaks up on you. Often characterized as a stirring adventure fantasy, you enter "Middle Earth" expecting a light, entertaining escape. Soon, however, your mind is stretching, your heart has upped its tempo and your inner sight is clearer.

While Tolkien has repeatedly denied that his story is more than just an enjoyable tale spun by an imaginative, skillful storyteller, he will admit to its being an "application" of the high principles of Christianity.

In Bilbo Baggins the plain and simple Hobbit who wanted little more than to be left alone, we see the fantastic capacity for greatness that frequently lies long unused in the most common and ordinary of us.

When Bilbo kills the giant spider with his small sword, a new confidence and resolution steals into his soul, and he is able to rescue his friends not once, but time and again. It illustrated for me the importance of success and the reinforcement it gives to our attitude.

As the story leaps from adventure to adventure, we can see the tempering of character and the hardening of spirit that is brought by adversity to Bilbo and Frodo.

Before Part I is over we see clearly the leadership that comes from competence, as the nonassuming little hobbit becomes the one to whom even the arrogant dwarfs look for help when the situation threatens.

The Hobbit and his companions show us that our greatest battles are often with anticipated terrors and not with the actual dangers themselves.

All in all, this is a story that excites and stimulates the imagination, galvanizes the reader's creativity, leaves clear examples of the conflict of forces going on all around us and inspires us to dare great adventures.

The Shadow of the Broad Brim

by Richard Ellsworth
Recommended by R. Herbert Fitzpatrick, Pastor
Upper Marlboro, Maryland

My favorite is *The Shadow of the Broad Brim*, which is a biography of Charles Haddon Spurgeon. Biographies have always been a great inspiration to me and I found them very valuable to my own spiritual growth.

It is interesting to study the lives of men that God has used and to see how God uniquely uses individuals with such varieties of personality and talent. Of course, knowing the author of any book personally makes the book far more interesting. I sincerely think this book would be of great value to anyone who would read it.

Following are excerpts from the above-mentioned book which are meaningful to me:

"We have plenty of people nowadays who could not kill a mouse without publishing it in a newspaper. Samson killed a lion and said nothing about it: the Holy Spirit finds modesty so rare that He takes care to record it. Say much of what the Lord has done for you, but say little of what you have done for the Lord. Do not utter a self-glorifying sentence! – C.H.S."

"Elijah's servant went once, and saw nothing; therefore he was commanded to look seven times. So many of you look lightly upon the Scripture and see nothing; meditate often upon it, and there you shall see a light like the light of the sun. – Joseph Caryl (1647)."

"I pray God, if I have a drop of blood in my body which is not His, let it bleed away. – C.H.S."

"God does not prolong the lives of His people that they may pamper themselves with meat and drink, sleep as much as they please, and enjoy every temporal blessing; but to magnify Him. – John Calvin."

The Fourth Dimension

by Dr. Paul Yonggi Cho
Recommended by: Dale E. Galloway,
Pastor, Portland, Oregon

The Fourth Dimension is a book that has literally changed my life. In two ways, I'll never be the same.

When I first read the book, it was at a time when all my lifetime goals, pursuits, and dreams were being fulfilled. I felt like a man who had nothing else to accomplish. Then I read *The Fourth Dimension*. As I read this book, God enlarged my vision to new horizons beyond anything I had ever dared to dream were achievable. If you are an achiever, reading this book will make you a greater achiever.

The second thing that the book did for me was that it created a deep thirst within me to learn how to fellowship with the Holy Spirit on a daily basis. I came to see clearly that it was only by being daily plugged into the greater power that the greater works that Jesus promised us that we would perform in John 14:12 would become a common reality in my life and ministry. If you've ever pondered and wondered about these words of Jesus, "Verily, verily, I say unto you, he that believeth on me, the works that I do shall he do also; and greater works than these shall he do; because I go to my Father," then you need to read *The Fourth Dimension*.

In my opinion, a great book is not a book that you read once and put down. What marks a book as outstanding compared to other books is that you find yourself going back to it for reference and inspiration and motivation, not just once but again and again. I found that *The Fourth Dimension* is that kind of book for me.

He that Is Spiritual

by Lewis Sperry Chafer
Recommended by: Alden A. Gannett,
Chancellor, Southeastern Bible College

Without a doubt, the book that has helped me most is *He that Is Spiritual*, authored by the founder and first president of Dallas Theological Seminary. What ministered to me especially was Lewis Sperry Chafer's clarity and simplicity in presenting how to live a victorious, fruitful Christian life – all from the Scriptures.

After stating clearly that our entrance into God's family is simply by trusting Christ to be our Savior (Eph. 2:8,9), he carefully distinguishes the baptism of the Spirit from the filling of the Spirit. The baptism of the Spirit, he explains, is the placing of the believer into Christ, and in turn, into the Church, the Body of Christ (1 Cor. 12:13). To be filled with the Spirit, he adds, "is to have the Spirit fulfilling in us all that God intended Him to do when He placed Him there."

The *How?* First, "Grieve not the Spirit" (Eph. 4:30), that is, confess all known sin to God; secondly, "Quench not the Spirit," or stop saying "no" to God (1 Thess. 5:19); and finally, "Walk in the Spirit," an unbroken reliance upon the Spirit – by faith one step at a time.

And the glorious results: on the one hand, victory over the world, the flesh and the devil; and on the other, the fruit of the Spirit: love, joy and peace. You can't beat that.

No teaching has helped me more.

Seek ye the Lord while he may be found, call ye upon him while he is near.

— Isaiah 55:6

The One Minute Manager

by Kenneth Blanchard and Spencer Johnson
Recommended by: Bill Glass,
Evangelist, Author, Former Pro Football Star

One of the most thought-provoking books that I have read in recent years is *The One Minute Manager*. On the cover there is a subtitle that reads: "a gem — small, expensive and invaluable." How true! The book is brief, and should be read several times. It is a gem of a great value!

It begins with a bright young man who is seeking to find an effective manager. The search is totally frustrated until he meets a "One Minute Manager."

This amazing manager is concerned about people and results. He has a plaque that reads: "People who feel good about themselves produce good results." The *One Minute Manager* tries to catch people doing the right thing. He wants to reinforce good results, just as a child showing even minor progress is praised highly, encouraging him to continue. Most managers wait to praise only that which is exactly right. But the baby that is even close is praised. That is why he progresses so fast.

He pursues the secret to management through three stages — one minute goal-setting, one minute praising, and one minute reprimand. All of these are vital and must be kept in equal balance in order to produce the most effective manager. It is filled with pithy statements like "take a minute," "look at your goals," "look at your performance," and, "see if your behavior matches your goals."

The Taste for the Other

by Gilbert Meilaender
Recommended by: Dave Grant,
Certified Professional Speaker, Author

Gilbert Meilaender's book, *The Taste for the Other,* has pulled together much of the social and ethical thought from the many writings of C. S. Lewis.

As Plato said, "We are discussing no trivial subject, but how a man should live." What I have learned from C. S. Lewis has helped me to live better. Here are a few examples:

Our Attitude toward Things: Life is seen as a constant movement back and forth between enjoyment and denunciation. The things of creation are intended to arouse delight without fully satisfying desire. We must love them enough to enrich our lives while we have them – not enough – to impoverish our lives when they are gone. Offer neither worship nor contempt.

Human Value: The infinite value of each human soul is not a Christian doctrine. God did not die for man because of some value He perceived in him. The value of each human soul considered simply in itself, out of relation to God, is zero. He loves us not because we were lovable, but because He is love.

The Journey of Life: It is a work of grace. Only a good man could really make the journey. Only a bad man needs to make it. The worse you are, the more you need it and the less you can do it. The only person who could do it perfectly would be a perfect person – and he would not need it. Christ therefore walks the path, retracing – this time with perfect obedience – the steps of Adam, – and all others do it only with His help.

The Lords of the Earth

by Don Richardson
Recommended by: Lorin Griset
Former Mayor, Santa Ana, California

One of the most thought provoking books I have read is *The Lords of the Earth,* by Don Richardson. It's the story of a man who fought the Japanese in New Guinea; then, after becoming a Christian, he dedicated himself to taking the Gospel of Jesus Christ to the people of New Guinea. As a single man who had been trained in jungle warfare, he was peculiarly equipped to endure the rigors of life in the remote areas of New Guinea where white men had never been. He was motivated not by a desire to kill, but by a desire to bring the message of life and love through Jesus Christ. He dared to go to people whose language he didn't know and who were known to kill for no apparent reason. After working alone for several years he met and married a missionary who shared his life. Children were born to them. After he established a "bridgehead" in a new area his family would join him.

This book is filled with the adventures of a man going into the unknown, possessing a firm conviction of faith in a God who would not fail. Some might say he was foolish, but he didn't think so. Even when he was flown out with 42 spear holes in his body, he recovered to go back and to ultimately be killed by primitive tribesmen. Today these tribesmen have become a Christian nation, transformed by the message that Stan Dale was first to bring. The book represents the most profound story of commitment and faith that I have read.

"O give thanks unto the Lord." — *Psalm 105:1*

Ethics of Freedom

by Jacques Ellul
Recommended by: Vernon Grounds,
President Emeritus of Conservative Baptist
Theological Seminary

I look for books to broaden my vision and sensitize my spirit to the problems and needs around me. The best books remind me that, despite technological transformation and increasing knowledge, human life and human nature do not change. There are a few basic verities, and these shine through good books which recall me to the essentials.

Jacques Ellul's *Ethics of Freedom* is the most probing analysis of the subject I've come across. Ellul examines political freedom, but also talks about working it out in all human relationships. In a kind of dialogue with the Bible, he relates the Christian concept of freedom as rooted in the liberating work of Christ. It's an original and brilliant work that I've found of practical value in implementing freedom in my own life.

I've found that biographies encourage and reinforce me in my daily struggles. I feel uplifted when I realize other Christians confront the same dilemmas and maintain consistent discipleship through them.

"Thy word is a lamp unto my feet, and a light unto my path."

—*Psalm 119:105*

The Jesus Style

by Gayle Erwin
Recommended by: John Haggai,
Evangelist, Author

Gayle Erwin's book, *The Jesus Style*, most influenced my thinking during the past year.

Erwin's thoroughly Biblical concepts, though hardly in vogue, explode in the mind and heart. One can read this book for two minutes, then think for two hours . . . or two days.

Here are a few of his conceptual time bombs:

"We make so few genuine decisions in life. Most of the choices we make are effected by outside forces and demands. But when it comes to the most important decision in life – our decision about God – He seeks only a genuine one. . . . God refuses to violate our personhood and our power to choose. That is love.

"Manipulation permeates our relationships with each other. . . . The chief means of resisting manipulation is humility – knowing who we really are and facing it."

Erwin points out that manipulation "destroys our ability to choose." And that, he insists, is a violation of personhood.

Then, this blockbuster: "To be a manipulator is to be a sick person." When we permit manipulation, we reinforce the manipulator's sickness. When we refuse, no matter how stormy the scene created by the manipulator, we contribute to his health.

You cannot read this book and be the same. It will force a response, whether positive or negative. I'm grateful to God and indebted to Erwin for the courage and love required to write *The Jesus Style* – in the Jesus style.

If God Is in Charge

by Stephen Brown,
Recommended by: Tom Haggai, CPAE,
Chairman of IGA

"I am learning, however, before I buy the book, go to the conference, subscribe to the magazine or begin a new program of self-improvement, to remember that God has not called me to be responsible for everything. I am learning by His grace, that growth is a gradual process, and that I don't have to be responsible now for being where I will be ten years from now.

"The rebel, with or without a cause, is often the hew of the myths and fiction of our culture.

"Because there are some things that finite human beings cannot understand, I believe God entered time and space to make a nonverbal statement. He didn't come to keep us from suffering; He came to suffer as we must suffer. He didn't come just to keep us from being afraid; He came to be afraid as we are afraid. He didn't come just to keep us from dying. He came to die as we must die. He didn't come to keep us from being tempted; He came to be tempted as we are."

The eyes of the Lord are in every place, behold-ing the evil and the good.

—Proverbs 15:3

My Utmost for His Highest

by Oswald Chambers
Recommended by: Richard C. Halverson,
Chaplain, United States Senate

Nine months after I met Jesus Christ, a copy of *My Utmost for His Highest,* by Oswald Chambers, was given to me for Christmas, 1936. On January 1, 1937, I began to read this daily devotional book, and with relatively few exceptions it has been my daily spiritual nurture ever since. One year I put it aside and experimented with several other daily devotionals, but they did not satisfy me.

No book except the Bible has influenced my walk with Christ at such deep and maturing levels. Nor has any influenced my preaching and teaching so much.

The book's strength lies in its stubborn insistence on the objective reality of redemption as the only secure foundation. Today subjective experience is often accepted as the criterion for authentic faith. In Chambers I am constantly being reminded that the ground of faith and experience is the person of Jesus Christ.

Chambers makes the point that Christian faith is rooted in events. The historicity of the gospel is its validation. Propositional truth is important, but the basis of faith is always Jesus Christ Himself.

Through the years Chambers has kept me on course by bringing me back to Jesus. Believing Jesus, not just believing my beliefs about Jesus, is basic.

God's Smuggler

by Brother Andrew
Recommended by: Jack Hartman,
Insurance Executive, Author, Teacher

I happened to come across a book titled *God's Smuggler* by Brother Andrew. This book told about a young Dutchman, Brother Andrew, and several trips that he took to Communist countries. On his first trip to Poland, Andrew was amazed to see the scarcity of Bibles behind the Iron Curtain and the tremendous black market prices that people paid for Bibles when they could get them.

On his next trip, he brought some Bibles with him and gave them away. They were eagerly received. This started a series of trips to Communist countries throughout Europe and also to Communist China. *God's Smuggler* tells specific, exciting stories of miracle after miracle which enabled Andrew to get Bibles through border checkpoints, keep his automobile running when mechanics said that it was impossible and to successfully escape from Communist soldiers with machine guns.

The book tells several fascinating stories about the underground church in Communist countries. It clearly shows the hunger that these Christians have for the Bible. The thoroughly documented miracles that occur throughout this book are a tremendous testimonial to the results of faith in God.

This book inspired me to study the Bible day and night and to put its instructions into practice in my life. As a result, I not only escaped bankruptcy, but our business is prospering greatly. Also, a Bible study class which started in our business office has now grown into a church with almost 1,000 people in attendance every Sunday morning.

Not Made for Defeat

by Douglas Hall
Recommended by: Warren Heckman,
Pastor, Madison, Wisconsin

Anyone who attempts great things for God will surely experience great trials in serving God. A modern-day example of this truth is Oswald J. Smith, founding pastor of The People's Church, Toronto. His life, ministry, commitment and integrity have challenged my life repeatedly. Douglas Hall captures the important ingredients of this energetic, innovative and inspiring man of God.

Oswald Smith is known and loved world-wide as a missionary, statesman, pastor, evangelist, Bible teacher, author and hymn writer.

On many occasions, Smith was unjustly criticized, attacked and openly ridiculed by certain newspapers. He lived by his most cherished motto, "No attack . . . no defense." Regardless of who urged him to rise up and answer the accusations, he absolutely refused. He left it all with the Lord, only determining to work harder for the Lord.

God has not called us to defeat, nor made us for defeat. Oswald Smith's life encourages everyone to discover God's purpose for their life and then "Go for it."

For what shall it profit a man, if he shall gain the whole world, and lose his own soul?
—Mark 8:36

Another Chance . . . How God Overrides Our Big Mistakes

by Dean Merrill
Recommended by: Roger L. Helle,
Director, Teen Challenge

Failure! So much of what many Christian counselors deal with is failure. And so many people who have taken a wrong turn in their life, feel that they can never get back into God's grace again. Somehow they feel that God cannot, nor will not, forgive them because they should have known better.

Does God forgive us? Will we ever get "another chance," when we have literally "blown it" and paid a tremendous price for our failure? What about the Pastor who has an affair which the deacon board exposes? Or the young women who has been raised in the church, and gets caught embezzling from the bank where she works? Or an unmarried teacher who bears a child or a policeman who gets caught operating on the wrong side of the law?

These are just a few of the true-to-life hurts that author Dean Merrill handles in his book, *Another Chance*. God is a God of "new beginnings." He is the Master Builder and He delights in resurrections. Only He can reconstruct a broken life and rebuild shattered dreams. In a world where people wander aimlessly with little or no direction and little or no HOPE, God has the answers.

Without hope, we are nothing, and we have nothing. But in Jesus, that hope is renewed. Our life does not have to be a self-condemning existence where we feel that "we blew it, and from now on we must suffer." Although Moses and David were both failures in the eyes of the world (both were murderers and David was an adulterer), yet by the power of God they rose up out of the ashes of their failure to become mightly men of God.

Quiet Talks on Power

by S. D. Gordon
Recommended by: Dr. Max Helton,
Pastor, Educator, Bakersfield, California

Quiet Talks on Power has a special appeal for those desiring to live life at its fullest.

"Every man needs power. Every earnest man covets power. Every willing man has the Master's promise of power. But every man does not possess the promised power. And many, it is to be feared, never will. Many a man's life today is utterly lacking in power. Some of us will look back at the close of life with a sense of keen disappointment and of bitter defeat. And the reason is not far to seek, nor hard to see through."

Meaningful to me was the realization brought by this book that there is available to me a fresh supply of power daily. I am glad that I discovered this early in life and am grateful to the person who shared this book with me. The author of this classic makes it clear that power is available to all. Pouring through its pages are thoughts that flood my mind with today's potential made reality that I am a channel through which flows rivers of living water.

The results of this power are given in the book as, "changes in the personality which attend the Spirit's unrestrained presence. Without a doubt the face will change, though it might be difficult to describe the change. That Spirit within changes the look of the eye. That new dominant purpose will modulate the voice, and the whole expression of the face, and the touch of the hand, and the carriage of the body. And yet the one changed will be least conscious of it, if conscious at all. Neither Moses nor Stephen knew of their transfigured faces." Power that transforms life. Power to live life at its fullest. Such a life is fragrance in the very presence of God.

The Seven Laws of Teaching

by John Milton Gregory
Recommended by: Dr. Howard Hendricks,
Professor, Dallas Theological Seminary

A book I recommend that has influenced my life is, *The Seven Laws of Teaching*.

. . . "the child is but a germ – he has not his destined growth – and he is ignorant – without acquired ideas. On these two facts rest the two notions of education: (1) the development of capacities, and (2) the acquisition of experience.

"True skill kindles and keeps alive enthusiasm by giving it success where it would otherwise be discouraged by defeat. The true worker's love for his work grows with his ability to do it well. Enthusiasm will accomplish all the more then guided by intelligence and armed with skill.

"Men's words are like ships laden with the riches of every shore of knowledge which their owner has visited; while the words of the child are but toy boats on which are loaded the simple notions he has picked up in his brief experience.

"This, then, is the Law of the Lesson: The truth to be taught must be learned through truth already known.

"Excite and direct the self-activities of the pupil, and as a rule tell him nothing that he can learn himself.

"True teaching, then, is not that which gives knowledge, but that which stimulates pupils to gain it.

"It is only the unskilled teacher who prefers to hear his own voice in endless talk rather than to watch and direct the course of the thoughts of his pupils.

"Even in the best-studied book, we are often surprised to find fresh truths and new meanings in passages which we had read perhaps again and again – The familiar eye discovers in any great masterpiece of art or literature touches of power and beauty which the casual observer cannot see."

Moving Heaven and Earth

by Donald F. Acklund
Recommended by: Frank W. Hewett, Col., USAF
Retired; President, Unified Systems Group, Inc.

Moving Heaven and Earth tells the story of Robert G. LeTourneau's life. I first met Mr. LeTourneau in the late 1940s when he spoke at our church on one of his many weekend trips from Peoria. At the time, I was working for a heavy equipment manufacturer and we were designing and building the same kind of equipment as LeTourneau. I was very impressed with the simple faith and honesty that was demonstrated by Mr. LeTourneau as he told me of his relying upon God to participate in every aspect of his life and work. It was considerably later, in 1957, that I met him again and purchased this book. He autographed it and wrote in Matthew 6:33 as a Scripture verse guiding the relationship of our temporal and spiritual lives.

"My philosophy is very simple. There are two things I like to do. One is to design machinery, turn on the power, and see it work. The other is to tell people about the power of the Gospel and see it work in their lives. Jesus was willing to become poor, that we, through His poverty, might become rich. So, for any success I have had, I humbly thank God."

As an engineer and a designer I have also found that God is abundantly able to provide assistance in the solution of technical problems. This is not a leverage relationship but an honest recognition that what I have and know is only because of the abundant grace of a loving Lord Jesus Christ.

Still Higher for His Highest

by Oswald Chambers
Recommended by: Don Hill,
President, Rowland Hill, LTD, Canada

It is a great thing to tell yourself the truth. If you are serious about being a Christian you need to read Oswald Chambers.

Behind every word is obviously a renewed mind, a yielded body and a captured heart resulting in a free spirit available for these great thoughts from God the Holy Spirit, to be put down for our gleaning and learning.

He speaks forthrightly to the heart. For example; "think what we shall feel like when we see Him if all the 'thank you' we gave Him for His unspeakable salvation was an obstinate determination to serve Him in our own way, not His."

It all starts with "Come unto Me". "God can do nothing for me if I am sufficient for myself."

Oswald's writings are constantly compelling the reader to check up on himself and see if his Christian life is real or just words.

"Christ asks me to give up the best I have got to Him, my right to myself." Christ our Example, gave up His rights as God, though God He remained, in order to become Man, the way that He as God created man to be. Then He gave up His rights as man, having lived a perfect life and therefore deserving Heaven, in order to experience hell (separation from God) on your behalf and mine. If that doesn't deserve a thank you, I quit. Hence, "let Me realize Myself in you."

"'He poured out His soul unto death' and that is to be the characteristic of our lives."

If you're interested in becoming rooted and built up in Christ Jesus, reading and absorbing Oswald Chambers will go a long way in producing an atmosphere in your life for this to take place.

Understanding Christian Missions

by J. Herbert Kane
Recommended by: Dave Hillis,
Dean, Washington Bible College

Books and materials claiming to equip the willing servant for overseas work are prolific. But they have not always fulfilled their promise.

One of the finest books for missionary education and training is *Understanding Christian Missions.* It is both practical and creative. Its historical references and biographies are encouraging, not boring.

Since my entire adult ministry has been in Australia and the South Pacific and most of my childhood was spent in India and Central America, I am especially concerned that texts used in Christian schools for studying missions should not suggest an "ivory tower approach." This book provides a fine balance between the academic and the useful. Some of the pitfalls we faced as pioneer missionaries and then as field directors of a national region, could have been avoided if we had known some of the insights this veteran servant of God and author had learned.

This book was not life-changing for me but it has become a valuable tool for understanding how a working missionary actually lives. Like a military front-line fighter, I appreciate tools that work! In so many battles the servants of God lack not theological or spiritual reference and knowledge but practical insights and experience. This book has been a dynamic encouragement to me as a missionary, teacher, and now as an administrator.

Preaching and Preachers

by D. Martyn Lloyd-Jones
Recommended by: Herschel H. Hobbs,
Pastor

I look for books that challenge me with positive truths about Christianity and faith. We hear too much of the negative – speakers and writers singing their doleful jeremaids about the decline of church and faith. Such books seldom bring out anything new; they simply restate old facts in new words. The mark of a good book, for me, is that it has a depth of scholarship to challenge the thinking believer. At the same time, it should be written in positive understandable language, which puts it in the domain of every reader, regardless of educational experience.

A book I've found very helpful in my preaching ministry is *Preaching and Preachers* by D. Martyn Lloyd-Jones. The author, an Englishman, gives us a thorough study of the art of preaching. It develops with candor and insight the preparation and delivery of sermons, the congregation and how it should be regarded, and the careful use of imagination and illustrations. In one section dealing with preparation for the preacher, Lloyd-Jones discusses reading. He says the preacher should not read to help himself think. "What we preach is to be the result of our own thoughts. We do not merely transmit ideas."

> . . . *a man's life consisteth not in the abundance of the things which he possesseth.*
> —*Luke 12:15*

George Muller, Man of Faith & Miracles

by Basil Miller
Recommended by: Clarence W. Hottel, Sr.,
Chairman, Fidelity Engineering Corporation

A book that helped me many times in the past to know how to be sure, was the story of a man, George Muller, who dared to believe God for miracles. Mr. Muller is one of the greatest prayer warriors of the past century and his biography has meant much to me for many years, particularly in the way he sought to know the will of God. The following six points have been his guide, which I try to follow:

"1) I seek at the beginning to get my heart into such a state that it has no will of its own in regard to a given matter.

2) Having done this I do not leave the result to feeling or simple impressions. If so, I make myself liable to great delusions.

3) I seek the will of the Spirit of God through or in connection with the Word of God. The Spirit and the Word must be combined.

4) Next I take into account providential circumstances. These plainly indicate God's will in connection with His Word and Spirit.

5) I ask God in prayer to reveal His will to me aright.

6) Thus through prayer to God, the study of the Word and reflection I come to a deliberate judgement."

Deeper Experiences of Famous Christians

by James Gilchrist Lawson
Recommended by: Dr. Curtis Hutson,
Editor, The Sword of the Lord

A book that has been a blessing and help to my life is *Deeper Experiences of Famous Christians.*

In essence, the book gives insights into the spiritual secrets of some very famous Christians. The unusual success of many of these Christians motivated me to set higher goals and attempt to reach more souls for Christ. I discovered that many of their secrets also worked for me. The secrets were nothing more than finding Bible principles and putting them into practice. I have often said that men are inspired by our example and instructed by our words. The example of these spiritual Christians gave me inspiration, their success gave me motivation, and the secrets gave me information as to how I could be a more successful Christian.

"The great object of this book is to describe, in their own words so far as possible, the deepest spiritual experiences of the most famous Christians of all ages and Times. The author has spent much of his time for years in the greatest libraries of Europe and America, searching the whole range of Christian literature to glean from it the most spiritual and helpful Christian experiences. He believes that this book contains the very cream of the Christian literature of all ages, and trusts that it will be the means of leading many into 'the fulness of the blessing of the gospel of Christ' (Romans 15:29)."

H. A. Ironside and Books

While Harry had put aside the thought of any more formal education, he continued to educate himself with books. He was, as he is now, an omnivorous reader, and at an early age had a fair-sized and good library, making up in quality what it lacked in quantity. Almost as familiarly to him as his Bible were the writings of famed poets and philosophers. Dickens, Longfellow, Kant, Plato, and other names marked his bookshelves. Bunyan's *Pilgrim's Progress* was read more than twenty times. Emerson was about the only essayist who left him indifferent. At the same time Harry was studying Chinese, for while at school he had met a Chinese doctor, and they used to spend two hours each week in mutual exchange of the English and Chinese languages. This interest in that old Oriental language has never left Ironside, and today he is able to make use of the tongue and the intricate characters with considerable facility for an Occidental who has never visited China. It was his ambition as a young man to come to know everything that is worth knowing, and he pursued his private studies to that end.

"Be of good courage, and he shall strengthen your heart."

—Psalm 31:24

The Secret Kingdom

by Pat Robertson
Recommended by: Jim Janz,
President, Crown Ambassador, Canada

Pat has been a great inspiration to me as he approaches life and the world in such practical terms.

In this book he is not trying to make people feel good but he is trying to give the solid God-inspired principles that give confidence to one's now and one's future.

For example:

"When a person has hope, when he knows his future is assured, he stops struggling to maintain his own sphere of dominance, he stops fighting other people. He is willing to let the law of God work to defend his place. Then he is free to have concern for the well being of others. He is no longer threatened and can give himself, his possessions, his life to someone else and know that God will make it right."

To understand the "Secret Kingdom" is to live in confidence and peace in a topsy turvey world. I thank God for men like Pat Robertson who say it like it is so that we can live life like it should be lived.

Blessed are they that hear the WORD OF GOD and keep it.

—Luke 11:28

Found: God's Will

by John MacArthur
Recommended by: Ken Johnson,
Christian Business Men's Committee of USA

God's will, according to MacArthur, is:

"1) That we be saved – truly have to be reborn into God's family.

2) That we are spirit-filled – that the Holy Spirit is controlling our life and we are letting Him continually fill us.

3) That we are sanctified – sanctified being translated to purity – purity of life. Living a life that is pure and set aside for the Lord.

4) That we be submissive. The apostle Paul wrote, "Submit yourselves to every ordinance of man, for the Lord's sake, whether it be to the king as supreme, or unto governors as unto them that are sent by Him for the punishment of evildoers, for the praise of them that do well for so is the will of God" I Peter 2:13–15.

5) That we would suffer – Peter states, "Rejoice in as much as ye are partakers of Christ's suffering" I Peter 4:13. Other Scripture relative to suffering is, "if ye be reproached for the name of Christ, happy are ye, for the spirit of glory and of God rests upon you . . . let none of you suffer as a murderer or as a thief or as an evildoer, or as a busybody under man's matters" I Peter 4:14–15. Mr. MacArthur states that suffering is par for the course for the Christian. Evangelism involves living a godly life in the face of an ungodly world and that will bring persecution because the world does not like Jesus."

Samuel Johnson and William Law

"This is the finest piece of hortatory theology in any language."

When at Oxford, I took up Law's *Serious Call to a Holy Life*, expecting to find it a dull book, (as such books generally are), and perhaps to laugh at it. But I found Law quite an overmatch for me; and this was the first occasion of my thinking in earnest of religion, after I became capable of rational inquiry. From this time forward, religion was the predominant object of his thoughts; though, with the just sentiments of a conscientious Christian, he lamented that his practice of its duties fell far short of what it ought to be.

How seriously Johnson was impressed with a sense of religion, even in the vigour of his youth, appears from the following passage in his minutes kept by way of diary: 'Sept. 7, 1736.' I have this day entered upon my 28th year. Mayest thou, O God, enable me, for Jesus Christ's sake, to spend this in such a manner, that I may receive comfort from it at the hour of death, and in the day of judgment! Amen."

"It is a good thing to give thanks unto the Lord."
—Psalm 92:1

Power through Prayer

by E. M. Bounds
Recommended by L. Johnston, President
Development Association for Christian Institutions

Since elaboration on its contents would most certainly dilute its impact, I refer the prospective reader to the following golden nuggets of truth found in its pages.

On education:

"No learning can make up for the failure to pray. No earnestness, no diligence, no study, no gifts will supply its lack."

On our present age:

"(This) age may be a better age than the past, but there is an infinite distance between the betterment of an age by the force of an advancing civilization and its betterment by the increase of holiness and Christ-likeness by the energy of prayer."

On "heads" vs. "hearts":

"He will use his intellect best who cultivates his heart most."

"Thought is not only brightened and clarified in prayer, but thought is born in prayer. We can learn more in an hour praying, when praying indeed, than from many hours in the study. Books are in the closet which can be found and read nowhere else. Revelations are made in the closet which are made nowhere else."

On the secret of power:

"No amount of money, genius, or culture can make more things for God. Holiness energizing the soul, the whole man aflame with love, with desire for more faith, more prayer, more zeal, more consecration—this is the secret of power."

That Incredible Christian

by A. W. Tozer
Recommended by: Gloria B. Jones,
Wife and Mother

My reading time has always been limited because of my busy life schedule. Therefore, I seek quality books that will be helpful in self-improvement, stimulation, and that motivate me to share with others. I found that *That Incredible Christian* by A. W. Tozer was a book of this nature.

One chapter that stands out in my mind most is the one that deals with Self-Judgment. The final judgment of the heart is God's. There is a sense in which we dare not judge each other and in which we should not try to judge ourselves. There is, nevertheless, a place for self-judgment and a real need that we exercise it. God already knows us thoroughly but it remains for us to know ourselves as accurately as possible. Here is Mr. Tozer's outline for self discovery. We may be known by the following:

What We Want Most
What We Think About Most
How We Use Our Money
What We Do With Our Leisure Time
The Company We Enjoy
Whom And What We Admire
What We Laugh At

These are a few tests. The wise Christian will find others.

That Incredible Christian is delightful reading with a message that calls for reflection and meditation.

I Dare You

by William H. Danforth
Recommended by: Jamie E. Jones,
Student, Liberty University

A book which has influenced my life greatly is *I Dare You*. It is completely filled with dares which William Danforth challenges us to accept. These dares are for those who are genuinely interested in developing both their inner and outer being to the fullest extent possible. Each of the author's dares will help us develop greater physical, mental, spiritual and social capacities, if we will sincerely commit ourselves to these challenges.

"The only reason you are not the person you should be is because you don't dare to be." Do we dare ourselves to be the best person we can possibly be? If not, we should be doing this daily. Our gifts need to be developed as much as possible. "Our most valuable possessions are those which can be shared without lessening: those which when shared, multiply. Our least valuable possessions are those which, when divided, are diminished."

There are four sleeping giants within us. They are the physical, the mental, the social, and the spiritual aspects of life. A life cannot be complete unless all four are developed. Each one that is developed touches the other three. Therefore, we have not one, but four lives to live. Strength and courage are essential to developing all four areas.

Finally, we are challenged to develop attitudes that will lead to accomplishing something notable. Rewards come to those who think hard, think often, and think creatively. Do not give up until you have released all your energy and shared your inner gifts with others. One spirit of this sort can set hundreds on fire. "And why dare? Because unless you dare you cannot win."

Perelandra

by C. S. Lewis
Recommended by: Jeffrey Jones,
Systems Test Engineer, Convex

I read *Perelandra* during junior high school. This book is the second of a science fantasy trilogy, and is by far my favorite of the three. The trilogy takes place on three different planets: Mars, Venus, and Earth. Perelandra itself is the planet Venus, and the story concerns the only two inhabitants of the planet, the King and the Lady, who live in beautiful gardens which cover the seas. They have been forbidden to live on the fixed land and have no desire to do so.

The devil's agent on Perelandra is an evil physicist called Weston, who has been sent to persuade the Lady of the joys of disobedience. Weston's arguments are subtle, convincing, and educational for the Lady. They are carefully crafted to illustrate certain points, while ignoring the flaws with which they are laden.

Playing counterpoint to Weston is another human, called Ransom, who is transported to Perelandra. Unsure of his purpose and seemingly overwhelmed by Weston, Ransom's arguments provide the only hope for steering the garden planet to the perfection it had been created for.

The allegories developed in *Perelandra* provide a fresh look at the present state of the world, and our hearts as well. It is a book well worth reading and rereading.

Oswald Chambers:
An Unbribed Soul

by D. W. Lambert
Recommended by: Jere J. Jones,
President, Executive Books

Oswald Chambers: An Unbribed Soul is a short, revealing look at the joys and sufferings behind one of the most popular devotional writers of our day.

D. W. Lambert looks at Chambers' youthful obsession with a career in the arts, his deep love of music and poetry, and his penniless early drifting. Particularly revealing in terms of Chambers' writing is the crisis of his twenties, while training for the ministry after having forsaken a career in art. In his quest for spiritual power, Chambers became so acutely aware of his self-righteous motivations for wanting that power, that he was driven to years of confused depression bordering on insanity. Lambert's focus on this early crisis, together with Chambers' later ministry in the midst of the suffering and death of World War I, give a new perspective regarding Chambers' repeated emphasis on the person of Christ.

Chambers never wrote a book for publication, yet over thirty volumes bear his name as author. Following his death in Egypt at age 43, Gertrude Chambers, who was only married to Oswald for seven years, spent the rest of her life editing the personal notebooks and outlines of devotional messages from Oswald's ministry. In addition to the portrait of Oswald, Lambert gives us a brief look at the woman who labored for 49 years after her husband's death to make us aware of his life.

Everyone who regularly reads Chambers' devotional writings should pause periodically to review this short look at his life in order to better appreciate his obsession with the life of Christ, as opposed to doctrine and gifts.

Holes in Time

by Frank Costantino
Recommended by: Rev. Max Jones,
Florida Prison Chaplain

These are some of the reasons I liked the above titled book:

Having worked with the State of Florida Department of Corrections for 20 years, I have met many people and have read many books—and I mean good books. However, even though I was used as an instrument of God to help Frank straighten out his life, the book he wrote was the first book written by an inmate I had ever read in which the author did not brag about his earlier life.

Bragging, even if unintentional, challenges the young people who read a book to do the same or do more.

Holes in Time was the first book I read that really revealed some of the inner workings of our Criminal Justice System. The system is revealed as a group of people, very professional, but still human and making mistakes as is true of all agencies. Some disreputable people infiltrate and cause much damage before being found out.

To me *Holes in Time* is the most thought-provoking book I have read. It is brutally true, yet at the same time warm and excitingly human.

Frank Costantino recently received a full pardon from the Governor of Florida and is instrumental in helping many others find what he found.

"Be ye doers of the word, and not hearers only."
—*James 1:22*

Hind's Feet on High Places

by Hannah Hurnard
Recommended by: Tracey Colleen Jones
Cadet, United States Air Force Academy

If I had to choose one book that I have continually turned to or one that has always stuck in the back of my mind as a reference or guide, it would be *Hind's Feet on High Places*. It deals with the universals of life, with man's struggle to overcome his own fears and deformities in his quest to reach new heights through the aid of his creator.

Throughout this book, the analogies to the Christians and their strivings to reach a communion with God are obvious readers of any age, and perhaps what makes this book so valuable.

Every human being, no matter what their background and walk of life can identify with the main character of Much-Afraid. Her continual struggles against her evil relatives, Pride, Resentment, and Craven Fear and her costly journeys through the Forest of Danger and Tribulations, and Valley of Loss are experiences that are common to us all. And yet, through the use of these analogies, Hurnard helps the reader to step back and see what is really there by stripping away all of life's distractions and simply presenting the continual battle that goes on for each man's soul. Much-Afraid's goal is like so many of our own — to reach the high places of a personal relationship with God through Christ. We can therefore read about her successes and failures and learn from them because they are such direct parallels to our own lives.

Adoniram Judson
Finds Direction through Reading

Unconsciously he was casting about for a direction to his life, watching for a sign. The sign appeared in September, when he had completed his first year at Andover. That month he came across a printed copy of a sermon which had aroused a great deal of interest in America. It was entitled "The Star in the East," and had been preached by a Dr. Claudius Buchanan not long before in the parish church in Bristol, England. Buchanan belonged to the evangelical school of the Church of England and had spent many years in India as a chaplain for the East India Company. He had taken for his text the part of the second chapter of Matthew which reads, "For we have seen his star in the East, and are come to worship him." Buchanan recounted how the gospel had been brought to India, and how it had progressed. He emphasized that the time was ripe to spread Christianity among eastern people by a greater effort than any up to this time. Most interesting to Adoniram, he told about the work of the beloved German missionary Schwartz, who had spent nearly fifty years teaching the gospel to the Indian heathen. As Adoniram, sitting alone in his little room, read Buchanan's stirring account with growing fascination, the stories of other pioneers must have risen to his mind.

Mrs. Adoniram Judson and Books

In May of 1805, however, when Nancy was fifteen — and five years before Adoniram met her — a new preceptor came to take charge of Bradford Academy. His name was Abraham Burham. Burham's influence soon began to be felt by the students, Nancy among them. At first the effect was so subtle, however, that she was not aware of what was happening to her. It first manifested itself one Sunday morning when she was dressing for church. On her dresser lay a copy of Hannah More's popular *Strictures on Female Education*. As she idly opened the book one italicized sentence caught her eye: "She that liveth in pleasure, is dead while she liveth." The line jumped out at her so startlingly that she felt as if an invisible power had brought it to her attention. Though the effect of the warning wore off after a while, she did not forget it. A few months later, reading Bunyan's *Pilgrim's Progress* as a "Sabbath book" she was struck by the final impression it left, "that Christian, because he adhered to the narrow path, was carried safely through all his trials, and at last admitted into heaven."

After a few days in this hostile frame of mind, however, her feelings began to alter as she considered the character of Jesus. She began to think that "God could be just, in saving sinners through Him." Reading Bellamy's *True Religion*, she came to accept God's hatred as a hatred of sin rather than sinners, and love for "the good of beings in general." She realized that she was beginning to have feelings and desires which were new to her and gradually had a hope that she "had passed from death unto life."

— Courtney Anderson

Beyond Humiliation, The Way of the Cross

by J. Gregory Mantle, D.D.
Recommended by: Robert J. Kelly
Co-publisher of the Pasadena Journal of Business

I found this treasure, in a barber shop, buried beneath a pile of tattered magazines.

In a few brief paragraphs, I was hooked. I bought several more to give to friends. I've read it again and again and, each time I do, it fills me with joy and hope, inspiration and challenge. I consider it an all-time great book, one to be read at least annually.

Of all the pure gold it contains, this passage is my favorite:

"Step by Step is the secret of a life which is never perturbed, never surprised by sudden assaults of the evil one, never shorn of its spiritual strength. With returning consciousness there is, in such a life, a resolute determination to take no step in the untrodden pathway of the day but by the Spirit. . . . Here is the principle by which our life is to be governed, and to follow it will fill our life with such joy and power as we never dreamed of before. . . . Our life is made up of these little steps. We fancy we could be heroic on some great occasion. We could die for Christ we think, if called upon to lay down our life for Him. It is questionable, however, if we could, unless we have cultivated the martyr spirit hour by hour, for if our strength and desire to please God have failed in the trifles of our life, how can we be sure of them in the great testing time? It is far harder to live for Christ moment by moment than it is to die once for Him; and if we wait for great occasions in which to display our fidelity, we shall find that our life has slipped away, and with it the opportunities which each hour has brought of proving our love to our Lord, by being faithful in that which is least."

Peace with God

by Billy Graham
Recommended by: D. James Kennedy,
Pastor, Fort Lauderdale, Florida

Peace with God, by Dr. Billy Graham, is a book which presents God's solution to the most important problem that mankind has ever faced: that of his own mortality, his own sin, his own failures and his own inevitable appointment with his Creator. If a person solves every other problem in this life but fails to solve this one, his life will, at its conclusion, have proved to be a tragedy as deep and as dark as can be woven from the warp and woof of mystery and death. *Peace with God* is a book which every immortal soul should read:

"Christ came to give us the answers to the three enduring problems of sin, sorrow, and death. It is Jesus Christ, and He alone, who is also enduring and unchanging, 'the same yesterday, and today and forever.'

"All other things may change, but Christ remains unchangeable. In the restless sea of human passions, Christ stands steadfast and calm, ready to welcome all who will turn to Him and accept the blessings of safety and peace. For we are living in an age of grace, in which God promises that whosoever will may come and receive His Son. But this period of grace will not go on indefinitely. We are even now living on borrowed time."

Executives

Jeremiah

Recommended by: Daryl Kraft
President, Environment Control Corporation

My favorite is *Jeremiah* (Bible Book). It's about a prophet who spent his entire life "cold calling" on potential customers, sharing His free service which promised total cleansing in exchange for repentance. However, very few accepted his offering, while most responded with hostility.

Here are just two of the anchors for my soul; nuggets that have been polished brighter with each reading and meditation:

PEACE is not a station I can ever arrive at in this life – it's a manner of traveling through this life. So if I can't find PEACE where I am, it's not to be found!

If God's Will is my greatest priority/desire – I'm in it! (In spite of what my circumstance may say.)

Christ at the Round Table

by E. Stanley Jones
Recommended by: Thomas F. Frederick
Palmer Memorial Chiropractic Clinic

Executives

How to Win Over Worry

by John E. Haggai
Recommended by: Mike Kubiatowicz,
President, Book Explosion

Victorious Christian Living

by Alan Redpath
Recommended by: Ben W. Jent,
President, Brady Energy

My Utmost for His Highest

by Oswald Chambers
Harry Hitchcock
retired

Spurgeon's Devotional Bible

by Charles Haddon Spurgeon
Recommended by: John M. Fisco, Jr.,
Chairman, ProBuColls

Temperament and the Christian Faith

by O'Hallesby
Recommended by: Tim LaHaye,
President, Family Life Seminars

Good books are such a meaningful part of my life that it is impossible for me to single out one book above all others as being the most thought provoking book I have read. I read by subjects and my interests are extremely varied.

One book that changed my life was *Temperament and the Christian Faith* by the Norwegian theologian O'Hallesby. Since then I have read twenty books on that subject and have written four of my own.

Dr. Francis Schaeffer has had a profound influence on my life and in opening my eyes to the secular humanist attack on society, the family and the church; particularly his books *How Shall We Then Live?*, *What Ever Happened to the Human Race?*, and *The Christian Manifesto*. I seriously question whether a Christian leader who has not read these books is capable of understanding why our culture is deteriorating and what Christians can do to change the direction of tomorrow. I was so moved by the first book mentioned I have written four books of my own on secular humanism.

There is Dr. David L. Cooper's masterful chart book on God's plan of the ages, *The Origin of Heathendom* and many others.

One book that stands out to me in recent years was ably written by Larry Richardson entitled *Eternity in Their Hearts*. As a veteran missionary, he put together the exciting story of how God has written in every tribe and language a message of the supreme God of the universe who loves man so much He has reached down to communicate with all men.

The Making of a Man of God

by Alan Redpath
Recommended by: Kenneth Larson,
President, Slumberland, Inc.

Redpath reminds us that the Bible never flatters its heroes with a single-sided view that only describes success and achievement. No doubt David was a great leader and a great king. But a complete look at his life includes being a shepherd, an exceptional soldier, an outlaw on the run, a hunted fugitive, a brilliant poet and a fallen sinner.

At the peak of David's career and his life, he slipped. As we reflect on David's sin, the author asks us to consider the relationship of this part of David to our own times. What saps the vitality of this country today? What undermines our national strength of character? What brings shame upon the Christian church? What causes more heartbreak than anything else in the world? It's the same sin of which David is guilty.

David's first impulse when conviction hit him was to run, and he ran for a year. But the second thought of a man of God is to return. David's heart and spirit had broken, and he declared his guilt and asked for forgiveness to God, and God honored his efforts.

This is a book of forgiveness and hope. It is a new look at challenge and purpose. *The Making of a Man of God* has had an impact on my thinking and my life.

Life More Abundant

by Charles Allen
Recommended by: Jack Leonard,
IBM, retired

Over the years I have read many books but one author that has been a great inspiration and help to me in my Christian life and walk is Charles Allen. His book *Life More Abundant* has meant a great deal to me. The following are excerpts which have been very helpful to me:

"When you decide God's way shall be your way, immediately you begin to walk. You stop worrying about whether you will fail or not; you just launch out on faith. There is a story of a young bear cub who was puzzled about how to walk. The little bear said to its mother, "Shall I move my right foot first, or my left, or my two front feet together, or the ones on the left side together and then the ones on the right side?" The mother bear said, "Leave off thinking about it and just walk."

We think about this problem and that one, about the future and where it might lead, and we get so confused we don't know which way to move. But when we say with Christ, "Thy will be done," we do see at least the first step and we find the strength to take that step. At this very moment say with me, "Now I yield my life to God's will, whatever His will may be." That is surrender, but surrender based on high faith and surrender that leads to complete victory. Phillipians 4:13 "I can do all things through Christ which strengthens me."

Jesus said, "No man can serve two masters." Until you choose your master, you will never have peace of mind.

How Should We Then Live

by Francis Schaeffer
Recommended by: Tom Lester,
Actor, "Green Acres" TV series

As I began to watch America deteriorate in the areas of religion, politics, the judiciary and the arts, I was puzzled as to why his was happening. I wondered why we had gotten so far away from our Biblical foundation.

After reading Francis Schaeffer's book, *How Should We Then Live,* and his excellent exploration of humanism and how this philosophy will destroy a civilization, I realized this was America's problem.

Humanism says that man is basically good and that he has the capacity to set his own standards of right and wrong with no absolute authority. Schaeffer shows how the Bible teaches that man has a fallen nature and so therefore does not have the capacity to set his own standard of right and wrong according to God's absolute. God's Holy Word must be the world's absolute authority.

Dr. Schaeffer also shows that as long as men and women in positions of responsibility make decisions from a humanistic base, we will continue to deteriorate as a nation. *How Should We Then Live* shows we must turn back to the absolute of God's Word or we as a race of people will continue to degenerate.

Greater love hath no man than this, that a man lay down his life for his friends.
—John 15:13

God's Workmanship

by Oswald Chambers
Recommended by: Capt. Bill Lewis USN (Ret)
Fellowship of Christian Athletes

In 1962 I was introduced to Oswald Chambers by a gift of *My Utmost For Highest*. God has blessed me with many other wonderful discoveries, but two of my favorites are *God's Workmanship* and *Imitation of Christ*. Here are a few of Chambers thoughts on grace:

"God is able to make all grace abound unto you; . . ." 2 Corinthians ix.8.

"In talking to people you will be amazed to find that they much more readily listen if you talk on the line of suffering, of the attacks of the devil; but get on the triumphant line of the Apostle Paul, talk about the super-conquering life, about God making all His Divine grace to abound, and they lose interest – 'That is all in the clouds', a sheer indication that they have never begun to taste the unfathomable joy that is awaiting them if they will only take it. All the great prevailing grace of God is ours for the drawing on, and it scarcely needs any drawing on. Take out the 'stopper' and it comes out in torrents; and yet we just manage to squeeze out enough grace for the day – 'sinning in thought, word and deed every day'! You don't find that note in the New Testament. We have to keep in the light as God is in the light and the grace of God will supply supernatural life all the time. Thank God there is no end to His grace if we will keep in the humble place. The overflowing grace of God has no limits, and we have to set no limits to it, but 'grow in grace, and in the knowledge of our Lord and Saviour Jesus Christ.'"

The Everlasting Man

by G. K. Chesterton
Recommended by: C. S. Lewis

"The contemporary book that has helped me the most is Chesterton's *The Everlasting Man*. Others are Edwyn Began's book, *Symbolism and Belief*, and Rudolf Otto's *The Idea of the Holy* and the plays of Dorothy Sayers.

"Now compared to these wanderers the life of Jesus went as swift and straight as a thunderbolt. It was above all things dramatic; it did above all things consist in doing something that had to be done. It emphatically would not have been done, if Jesus had walked about the world forever doing nothing except tell the truth. And even the external movement of it must not be described as a wandering in the sense of forgetting that it was a journey. This is where it was a fulfillment of the myths rather than of the philosophies; it is a journey with a goal and an object; like Jason going to find the Golden Fleece, or Hercules the golden apples of the Hesperides. The gold that he was seeking was death. The primary thing that he was going to do was to die. He was going to do other things equally definite and objective; we might almost say equally external and material. But from first to last the most definite fact is that he is going to die.

"From the moment when the star goes up like a birthday rocket to the moment when the sun is extinguished like a funeral torch, the whole story moves on wings with the speed and direction of a drama, ending in an act beyond words."

Loving God

by Charles Colson
Recommended by: George V. Lilja,
Football Player, Cleveland Browns

This book really brought me back to my first love. Not football or sports, rather my God and Savior, Jesus Christ.

"A friend urged me to watch Sproul's series. By the end of the sixth lecture I was on my knees, deep in prayer, in awe of God's absolute holiness. It was a life-changing experience as I gained a completely new understanding of the holy God I believe in and worship.

"My spiritual drought ended, but this taste of the majesty of God only made me thirst for more of Him. So I gathered up contemporary books on the subject of discipleship – by the armload. Many were excellent, though they often dealt more with evangelism than discipleship; and most seemed concerned with how to get more out of the Christian life. I wanted to know how to put more into it.

"One thing all the books dealt with, of course, was God's love for humanity and how He showed that love by the sacrifice of His Son on the cross. The more I read about this, the more I wanted to know about what I had begun to see as the corollary – how I show my love for Him. Somehow that seemed to be the key to putting more into the Christian life."

God commandeth His love toward us, in that while we were yet sinners Christ died for us.
—Romans 5:8

Spirit Controlled Temperament

by Tim LaHaye
Recommended by: Florence Littauer
Author, Professional Speaker

The one book that has influenced my life the most is Tim LaHaye's *Spirit Controlled Temperament*. At the time I read it 17 years ago, my husband Fred and I had recently committed our lives to the Lord after many years of a difficult marriage. I thought if he could only relax and have fun, I could be happy. He felt if only he could get me organized and on a chart, he could be happy. We both had been trying to shape each other up – it hadn't worked.

When I read *Spirit Controlled Temperament*, I found a concept as old as Hippocrates which explained why Fred and I were so different. I was a Sanguine, fun-loving, with a sense of humor. Fred was a Melancholy, deep, serious, and analytical. For the first time in our married life we began to understand each other and accept each other as we were.

As soon as we had read the book, Fred and I started teaching couples how to understand each other. We saw instant results and soon we were leading seminars on personality, followed ultimately by my writing *Personality Plus*, a book which has been used to change many more lives.

Never underestimate the power of the written word!

The Divine Library

by Henrietta C. Mears

The Old Testament is the foundation; the New Testament is the superstructure. A foundation is of no value unless a building be built upon it. A building is impossible unless there be a foundation. So the Old Testament and New Testament are essential to one another.

"The New is the Old contained,
The Old is in the New explained.
The New is in the Old latent,
The Old is in the New patent."

The Old Testament and New Testament constitute a divine library, one sublime unity, origins in past to issues in future, connecting two eternities.

One Book, One History, One Story

The Bible is one book, one history, one story, His story. Behind 10,000 events stands God, the builder of history, the maker of the ages. Eternity bounds the one side, eternity bounds the other side, and time is in between – Genesis, origins, Revelation, endings, and all the way between God is working things out. You can go down into the minutest detail everywhere and see that there is one great purpose moving through the ages, the eternal design of the Almighty God to redeem a wrecked and ruined world.

The Bible is one book, and you cannot take it in texts and expect to comprehend the magnificence of divine revelation. You must see it in its completeness. God has taken pains to give a progressive revelation and we should take pains to read it from beginning to end. Don't suppose reading little scraps can ever be compensation for doing deep and consecutive work on the Bible itself. We must get back to the Book and then we will not tolerate such work. One would scorn to read any other book, even the lightest novel, in this fashion.

Things I've Learned

by Bob Jones, Sr.
Recommended by: Don Lonie,
Dean of American High School Speakers

The book that has meant the most to me and influenced my high school speaking the most is *Things I've Learned*, by the founder of Bob Jones University. Here are a few quotes which are as true today as they ever were.

"You don't get married with an escape clause in the marriage contract."

"Success comes to those who use good judgement. Take a good look at your life. You may live for 50 years. Don't sacrifice tomorrow on the Altar today. You are drivers or drifters. You decide what you want for your life or others decide for you."

"When it comes to reckless driving, it doesn't make any difference to God whether you are the high school bum or the high school athlete. In the case of an accident, He counts them all the same."

"Don't go any place where you can't go in the front door and come out the front door. This is the difference between character and reputation."

"Sex is not a toy; it is life-producing. There is a third party to the contract of sex, and His name is God!"

"Boys, don't defile yourself, and you won't defile your girlfriend."

Train up a child in the way he should go; and
when he is old, he will not depart from it.
—Proverbs 22:6

Fight: A Practical Handbook for Christian Living

by John White
Recommended by: Don Lykins,
Retired Businessman

John White has helped me present Christ in a way that fulfills the scripture where Paul says in Galatians 5:26 KJV, "Let us not be desirous of vain glory, provoking one another, envying one another."

"By a miracle of divine grace a nonbiological life was implanted in you. It is a form of life that will enable you one day to inhabit eternity just as your biological life now enables you to live in time-space."

"The life that entered you was the life of God himself. Your earthly parents gave life from their living bodies which became your life when you were born. In the same way God, in implanting to you His own life, became in very deed your Heavenly Father. You are a child of God in a literal, not a metaphorical sense."

"But the life must grow and develop, for your new life to grow. It must be fed and exercised. The food it requires is the Holy Scriptures. Exercise will consist of obedience by faith to the commands of God."

As time goes on you will become increasingly expert at discerning His voice and being able to follow wherever He leads.

Charles Malik and Books

Past President, United Nations Security Council
& General Assembly

It will take a different spirit altogether to overcome this great danger of anti-intellectualism. As an example only, I say this different spirit, so far as the domain of philosophy alone is concerned, which is the most important domain so far as thought and intellect are concerned, must see the tremendous value of spending a whole year doing nothing except poring intensely over the *Republic* or the *Sophistes* of Plato, or two years over the *Metaphysics* or the *Ethics* of Aristotle, or three years over the *City of God* of Augustine. Even if you start now on a crash program in this and other domains, it will be a century at least before you catch up with the Harvards and Tubingens and the Sorbonnes, and think of where these universities will be then! For the sake of greater effectiveness in witnessing to Jesus Christ Himself, as well as for their own sakes, the Evangelicals cannot afford to keep on living on the periphery of responsible intellectual existence.

For God so loved the world, that he gave his only begotten Son, that whosoever believeth in him should not perish, but have everlasting life.
—John 3:16

The Sovereignty of God

by Arthur W. Pink
Recommended by: Dr. Kenneth A. Markley,
Special Projects, Narramore Christian Foundation

After scanning the shelves in my study and selecting and rejecting countless volumes as the most influential book in my life, I finally settled on a masterpiece written in 1930 – about nine years before I was able to read or write – entitled, *The Sovereignty of God.* The author of this wonderful little book shared with me the life-changing concept of God's absolute rule in the life of man and the affairs of the universe. Nothing I have ever read or will discover in future readings could ever compete with Dr. Pink's clear and penetrating analysis of the Biblical truth of God's overruling control of every aspect of all things.

The following quotation from this great book hardly does justice to its integrated message. Perhaps it will serve to illustrate the thrust of Pink's purpose in writing it . . . to focus on God's sovereign grace in the lives of men:

"The sovereign election of certain ones to salvation is a MERCIFUL provision . . . (because), unless God has chosen certain ones to salvation, *none* would have been saved, for 'there is none that seeketh after God' (Romans 3:11). And be it noted, in choosing the ones He did, God did no injustice to the others who were passed by, for none had any *right* to salvation."

The doctrine of God's absolute sovereignty gives me peace, confidence, hope, and motivation to proclaim the gospel to all people so that God's elect ones will be drawn to Him and be saved.

Catherine Marshall and Books

"How can God permit such things to happen?" is the
cry that rises from our hearts. If He exists at all and
is a loving God, He would not want such evils to befall
us. Yet how could He be God and not have the power
to prevent these disasters? These are the most difficult
of all questions for those embarked on the Christian
walk. Certainly for me this problem of evil has been a
real stumbling block.

In my groping to understand, back in the forties
during a long illness I "discovered" a body of Christian
literature unknown to me. It was experiential, the true
personal experiences of other people. Compared to
most church literature which I knew so well – largely
theory – this was exciting reading. I gobbled up everything by A. B. Simpson, Glenn Clark, Starr Daily,
Rufus Mosley, Frank Laubach, Rebecca Beard,
Dorothy Kerin, Roland Brown, and later on C. S.
Lewis and Agnes Sanford. In addition, I began to
search out the journals and letters of some who had
lived in other eras – Brother Lawrence's *Conversations*. John Foxe, John Wesley, Hannah Whitall Smith,
George Muller, Evelyn Underhill. These journals and
letters proved a rich mine of personal experience.

Peter Marshall

Pastor, Former Chaplain, United States Senate

His favorites in literature were Shakespeare, Milton,
John Buchan, Robert Burns, F. W. Boreham (the Aus-
tralian), Leslie Weatherhead, George Buttrick, A. A.
Milne, and the King James Bible. He had been known
to mix any combination thereof in a sermon. Why
not? These were men and books he liked.

– Catherine Marshall

Tough Times Never Last, But Tough People Do

by Robert H. Schuller
Recommended by: Daniel F. May,
CEO, Republic Airlines, Inc.

Dr. Schuller's "possibility thinking" approach to coping with tough problems was a real source of strength to me. His challenge to solve the problems that can be solved and manage the problems that can't be solved is presented in a logical and inspiring manner. It is a book well worth reading.

"Let faith be in control of every decision you make and every action you take. You do that when you let the positive possibilities set your goals.

"When you look at your life and where it's headed, ask yourself these questions: 'Who's in charge? Who's in control? To whom have I surrendered leadership?'"

"Surrender leadership to faith. Surrender leadership to God. Let Him be in control of your life. Ask Him three questions: 'God, who am I? Why am I here? Where am I headed?' At the very least, His answers may surprise you. They will open your eyes to the beautiful person that you are and will become, as well as to the fantastic future that awaits you."

If ye love me, keep my commandments.
—John 14:15

How to Pray

by R. A. Torrey
Recommended by: W. S. McBirnie,
Pastor, Glendale, California

I remember after all these years the book that made a very great difference to me. Fortunately it is in paperback and still in print – available from the Moody Press, Moody Bible Institute, Chicago.

I was seventeen, a Bible college student, and a between terms missionary in Northern Saskatchewan during the summer of 1937. Among the people resettled on government-grant forested lands, because of the big drought of the 1930's – I went from cabin to cabin to spread the Word. I had two books with me, the Bible and R. A. Torrey's *How to Pray*.

To this day I think it is one of the best books I know because it really gets down to the fundamentals of how to pray and receive answers from God. I went to Canada as a boy and came back a man. I had learned some of the greatest secrets of Christianity and they are still the strength of my ministry as a pastor, Graduate School of Theology Professor, and daily Radio News Analyst on the Voice of Americanism.

Trust in the Lord with all thine heart, and lean not unto thine own understanding. In all thy ways acknowledge him, and he shall direct thy paths.

—Proverbs 3:5,6

Destined for the Throne

by Paul E. Billheimer
Recommended by: Jim McEachern,
C.E.O., Tom James Company

This book attracted me because of Bill Graham's foreword. This outstanding book related to "prayer, praise, and the church's place in the world."

During my life, I have observed that the happiest people in the world love God with all their heart, soul and mind; and they love their neighbors as themselves. The most miserable people in the world are self-centered.

"The quintessence of all our mental and nervous disorders is over-occupation with the personal ego; namely, self centeredness. When the personality becomes centripetal, that is ego-centered, it disintegrates. Out of extreme self-centeredness arises defensiveness, hostility, and aggressive anti-social behavior."

"To make one's self his center is self-destructive."

"Here is one of the greatest values of praise (of God): it decentralizes self. The worship and praise of God demands a shift of center from self to God. One cannot praise without relinquishing occupation with self. When praise becomes a way of life, the infinitely lovely God becomes the center of worship rather than the bankrupt. Thus, the personality becomes properly integrated and destructive stresses and strains disappear. This results in mental wholeness. Praise produces forgetfulness of self – and forgetfulness of self is health."

The Reason Why

by Robert Laidlaw
Recommended by: Bob McFarland,
Executive Sales Trainer

As we travel down life's road, there are many forks we face and the decision always exists as to which path to take. I had come to one of the many "forks" when a little book, *The Reason Why*, fell across my path. This little book, only 4 by 6 inches in size and 46 pages long, "turned me on," in the early morning hours, to read the Bible, a book that has more answers in it than anything else I have read and believe I ever will read. It's no wonder that over 20 million copies of *The Reason Why* have been printed in more than 30 languages and that thousands of lives have been influenced by its message.

"Every thoughtful person believes in a series of causes and effects in nature, each effect becoming the cause of some other effect. The acceptance of this as fact logically compels one to admit that there must be a beginning to any series. There could never have been a first effect if there had not been a first cause. This first cause to me is Deity. You know that where there is a design there must be a designer."

It takes little time to read *The Reason Why*, but it could be the reason why you, too, may start a reading habit that can affect the course your life may take – as it did mine.

Ecclesiastes

*Recommended by: R. Gordon McGovern, CEO
Campbell Soup Company*

A book that has been very inspirational to me is *Ecclesiastes* from the Bible.

Ecclesiastes is the teachings of a wise old preacher who says, in essence, make the most out of what God has given you. Don't be concerned with material things. My favorite passages are:

Chapter 12, 13th Verse:

". . . Fear God, and keep his commandments: for this is the whole duty of man."

Chapter 3, Verse 22:

". . . there is nothing than that a man should rejoice in his own works."

I also like the poetic passages that begin Chapter 3:

"To every thing there is a season . . .", etc.

The Mystery of Godliness

by Major W. Ian Thomas
Recommended by: R. L. McMillan, Insurance
Executive Recipient of the National Association of Life
Underwriters' John Newton Russell Award

I am an avid reader and it is very difficult to filter one book to the top in addition to the paramount one, the Holy Bible.

In *The Mystery of Godliness*, W. Ian Thomas vividly describes the law of the Spirit of Life in Jesus Christ, and he says:

1. He had to come as He did (miraculous birth) to be what He was (perfect).
2. He had to be what He was (perfect) to do what He did (redeem).
3. He had to do what He did (redeem) that you might have what He is (life).
4. You must have what He is (life) to be what He was (perfect).

God's capacity to reproduce Himself in us is a great mystery – the mystery of Godliness. The more I seek to know the nature of this mystery, the more wonderful it becomes and more thrilling is the search for it.

. . . Eye hath not seen, nor ear heard, neither have entered into the heart of man, the things which God hath prepared for them that love Him.
—1 Corinthians 2:9

Moses Mendelssohn and Books

"These ideas are not merely the fruits of hard thinking in which the heart has no share. No! I speak feelingly, I speak from a live conviction.

"Ask our friend . . . who handed you this letter. He knows how near I once was to a complete ruin. My feet slipped from the happy path of virtue. Cruel doubts in Providence tortured me like furies of hell; doubts even in the existence of God and in the worthwhileness of virtue, as I may confess to you without fear. I was ready to give rein to all base desires. Drunk with lust, I was in danger of falling into the abyss in which the slaves of vice descend to lower levels as the hours pass. Come on, despisers of the true philosophy! Come on, shallow thinkers who regard every profound reflection as absurd! Save a single soul from the jaws of perdition. Muster all faculties of your soul! Give good advice! What was I to do? Nip the rising doubts in the bud? By what means? Through Faith? Wretched me! I tried but can the heart believe when the soul is in doubt?

"You fall into silence? Your loquacity, which had an answer to everything, is all of a sudden at a dead end. Your specious arguments have evaporated into thin air, and you leave me to my misery? My thanks are due to the faithful guides who led me back to true knowledge and to virtue. To you Locke, and Wolff; to you immortal Leibniz, I set up an eternal memorial in my heart! Without your help I would have been lost for ever. I never met you in the flesh, yet your imperishable writings – which are unread by the world at large and which I implored for help in the hours of my loneliness – have guided me to the firm path of the true philosophy, to the knowledge of myself and of my origin. They have engraved upon my soul the sacred truths on which my felicity is founded; they have edified me."

The Christ Life

by A. B. Simpson
Recommended by: Rev. Tracy Culver Miller,
Pastor, Camp Hill, Pennsylvania

"The Christ-centered message of Albert B. Simpson, the founder of The Christian and Missionary Alliance is timeless. Breaking through the stereotypes of his day, Simpson preached the gospel with apostolic freshness. He had no time for the niceties of any closed theological system but drew from the wellsprings of the Scripture the truth that Christ is all and in all.

"The sum of his doctrinal system was that the believer is in Christ and Christ is in the believer and from that union comes all spiritual reality. *The Christ Life* is one of Simpson's best treatments of this emphasis. The book is uncomplicated and yet profound in its perspective of biblical Christology. Though written in devotional language, it is rich in doctrinal content."

HIMSELF, by A. B. Simpson
Once it was the blessing,
  Now it is the Lord;
Once it was the feeling,
  Now it is His Word.
Once His gifts I wanted,
  Now the Giver own;
Once I sought for healing,
  Now Himself alone.

Once I hoped in Jesus
  Now I know He's mine;
Once my lamps were dying,
  Now they brightly shine.
Once for death I waited,
  Now his coming hail;
And my hopes are anchored,
  Safe within the vail.

The Complete Library

by Charles Haddon Spurgeon

In case the famine of books should be sore in the land, *there is one book which you all have, and that is your Bible;* and a minister with his Bible is like David with his sling and stone, fully equipped for the fray. No man may say that he has no well to draw from while the Scriptures are within reach. In the Bible we have a perfect library, and he who studies it thoroughly will be a better scholar than if he had devoured the Alexandrian Library entire. To understand the Bible should be our ambition; we should be familiar with it, as familiar as the housewife with her needle, the merchant with his ledger, the mariner with his ship. We ought to know its general run, the contents of each book, the details of its histories, its doctrines, its precepts, and everything about it. Erasmus, speaking of Jerome, asks, "Who but he ever learned by heart the whole Scripture? or imbibed, or meditated on it as he did?" It is said of Witsius, a learned Dutchman, author of the famous work on "The Covenants," that he also was able, not merely to repeat every word of Scripture in the original tongues, but to give the context, and the criticisms of the best authors; and I have heard of an old minister in Lancashire, that he was "a walking Concordance," and could either give you chapter and verse for any passage quoted, or, *vice versa,* could correctly give the words when the place was mentioned. That may have been a feat of memory, but the study needful to it must have been highly profitable. I do not say that you must aspire to that; but if you could, it would be well worth the gaining.

A Life of Trust

by George Mueller
Recommended by: Sam Moore,
President, Thomas Nelson Publishers

The book that meant the most in my life was *A Life of Trust* by George Mueller. It came at a time when I needed it most and is a great book on faith and trust in God. I think I may have loaned out my last copy and it was my marked copy and I'm not sure I even remember who has it.

The essence of the book is simple – When you have faith in God, things happen to please Him in your life, it doesn't necessarily mean it goes to please us. As long as it is for the honor and glorification of God, that will be the will of God. As Job said, "Though He slay me, I will still love Him and serve Him", this is what the attitude of the Christian should be – to trust God in everything. That is why Romans 8:28-29 are so important. Roman 8:28 is so misunderstood by so many Christians today, they think that all things work together for good for the Christian. I think that verse means that all things work together for the good of the will of God in the life of that Christian and God is trying to accomplish things. This is my kind of "off the cuff" remark.

"Behold, I am with thee, and will keep thee."
—Genesis 28:15

John R. Mott and Books

1865–1955
YMCA Executive,
Recipient of Nobel Peace Prize – 1946

At Wooster he and Leila devoted themselves that autumn to an intensive study of the life of Christ, having procured eight of the newest biographies, including those by Edersheim, Farrar, Stalker, and Broadus, "a tremendous gold mine." John wrote to Hattie, who had asked him to recommend titles for a missionary library, but "nothing however when compared with the plain Gospel accounts." The books he and Leila were studying ran the gamut of current scholarship from German higher criticism to Southern Baptist evangelicalism; that they could derive both knowledge and spiritual sustenance from them not only evidenced her husband's irenic spirit that Leila was happy to embrace, but showed the influence of Mott's travel among the colleges. Loyalty to Jesus Christ was the guiding principle of his life, but he could not rely upon the impetus of the past to meet either his own needs or those of the increasing numbers of college youth who were looking to him for guidance and inspiration. Unlike Moody and other contemporary evangelists, Mott possessed a compulsion to read and to weave the best scholarship of his time into his message – a partial explanation of his growing popularity as an evangelist to students.

– C. Howard Hopkins

"For God is the King of all the earth."
– Psalm 47:7

Executives

Prophet to India

by Russell Olt
Recommended by: George Mowery, retired

The life of William Carey was especially meaningful
to me during my college years. The lives of John
Bunyan and Martin Luther are two others that I enjoyed.

The Indescribable Christ

by Charles Rolls
Recommended by: Donald M. Smith, retired

I recently made a fantastic discovery while reading
a book entitled *The Indescribable Christ*. My new discovery provides me with a simple and effective way of
expressing my Christian way of life that is acceptable
both to the Christian community as well as to the
world in general.

The key word is Goodness. Charles Rolls quotes a
verse from the Psalms to introduce this interesting
subject: "O give thanks unto the Lord for He is good."
He goes on to explain that, "because He (Christ) is
inherently good, He is able to make us good." Finally,
he explains the real meaning of goodness. To quote:
"Goodness is reasonable as well as righteous, it is
courteous as well as cautious, confident as well as
competent and graceful as well as grateful. Goodness
approves forgiveness and advocates it. We cannot conceive of one that is better and more complete than a
good person."

George Mueller and a Book

George edged forward in the overstuffed chair to read the titles of the books – Virgil, Cicero, Thackeray, Dickens. But what was this? From behind a leather-bound volume of poetry, a book slid off the shelf into his hand. It was the biography of Franke from Halle!

He stared down at it. He knew the book well. Already had read it twice, each time profoundly stirred by the faith of the man who had dared to go against eighteenth-century customs and build an orphanage. The man had had no money; he had simply asked God to send it to him, and God had.

Holding the book in his hand, George wondered how much it had influenced him to begin his own adventure with God. And now to meet it again, here in this house. It was also more than coincidence.

For the rest of the week he thought about nothing else. At the end of the week, he went to Henry Craik's study, and he confided in him a plan that was now fully shaped in his own mind. This was it: He would rent a cheap house right in the middle of Bristol. He would take any youngsters that needed a home, at least twenty or thirty, and feed them, clothe them, and educate them, as if they were his own family.

If God answered prayer in 1727 for Franke, He answers it in 1835 too.

"And all things, whatsoever ye shall ask in prayer, believing, ye shall receive."
—Matthew 21:22

1980 Countdown to Armageddon

by Hal Lindsey
Recommended by: John J. Mueller,
Soccer Player, St. Louis Stars, Cleveland Stokers

This is what it's all about:

"Communism is a Religion"
"To understand the communist mind and its motivations, you must first realize that communism is more of a religion than a political philosophy. It is a religion based on certain erroneous concepts of man and his nature.

"Communism believes that man has no soul. He secretes thoughts and a personality just as a stomach secretes digestive juices. Man is purely a material being whose nature can be shaped by his environment, the communists say. Change the environment and you change the man. This notion is diametrically opposed to Judeo-Christian thought.

"Marxist-Leninists believe that they have discovered the fundamental laws which shape men and history. The number one corrupter of mankind, they say, is capitalism and the free enterprise system. Private ownership of property and a competitive economic system make men selfish, greedy and aggressive, the communists, believe."

"When you see the Russian army begin to move southward and enter Turkey, put on your Sabbath garments and get ready to welcome the Messiah.
                                            —Rabbi Chaim Valoshiner,
                                               mid-19th century"

Living without Losing

by Don Polston
Recommended by: Carolyn Musser,
Business Executive, Princess House

I'm excited about the book, *Living without Losing*, by Don Polston. This book became my "friend" about 8 years ago, and I treasure its friendship to this day. I am enthused about its contents because it covers many phases of our everyday life, and gives counseling for our situations, based on "God's Love."

When this friend and I get together, we are able to contemplate such thoughts as: "Tips for Triumph," "The Test of a Man," "Ambition," "The Winning Wife," "Three Steps to Successful Living," "How to Increase Your Energy," "How to Have a Better Home," "Your Unrealized Possibilities," plus many other subjects.

I share these friendly chats at many of my sales meetings with other sales people. There has been growth in their lives as well, through these golden nuggets. I will treasure this friend for life.

There hath no temptation taken you but such as is common to man: but God is faithful, Who will not suffer you to be tempted about that ye are able; but will with the temptation also make a way to escape, that ye may be able to bear it.

—I Corinthians 10:13

The Sensation of Being Somebody

by Maurice E. Wagner
Recommended by: Clyde M. Narramore,
President, Narramore Christian Foundation

This book has been a blessing to me, not only because of its content, but because Dr. Wagner has been a close personal friend and colleague for many years.

As a matter of fact, he was the first therapist I brought to my staff over twenty years ago. He is a godly man, has a rich background both in theology and psychology, and is considered one of America's outstanding therapists.

This book is a classic in the area of building an adequate self-concept and is in its thirteenth printing now. It was first published in 1975. It was one of the first professionally written books intended both for lay persons as well as professional therapists, which also has a workbook suitable for individual or group study.

This book is totally consistent with Christian principles. Wagner explores what we are, how we have become what we are, and what we can become. I trust it will be a blessing to all who avail themselves of it.

"Whatsoever ye would that men should do to you, do ye even so to them."
—Matthew 7:12

Spiritual Leadership

by J. Oswald Sanders
Recommended by: Arthur Nazigian,
Headmaster, The Christian Academy

In what direction does one look to find a leader? So often Christian colleges and schools lament the fact that they are not producing enough leaders. As one examines the Word of God, he sees that God is looking for faithful servants . . . servants who are yielded and submissive to Himself and to their fellow man. From these servants, He will choose the leaders. It is no one's task to produce spiritual leaders.

Oswald Sanders begins his inspiring book by asking, "Should it not be the office that seeks the man, rather than the man the office?" Personal ambition is the arch enemy of everyone with leadership potential.

I liked the book because the principles shared were not only scriptural, but attainable. The author develops his thinking in such a clear way that one can implement the key truths outlined.

So often, natural ability is cited as the reason for leadership work well done, when it is simply the Hand of God upon a spirit-filled man. Saint Francis of Assisi was a key example of this. On one occasion, Brother Masseo, looking earnestly at Francis, said, "Why thee? Everyone follows thee, everyone desires thee, to hear thee, to obey thee and yet for all that, thou are neither beautiful, nor learned, nor of noble family."

The great and yet simple golden nuggets of insight are shared to lead the servant of God, bent on serving Him, to realize that in our service . . . we lead others!

There never was found, in any age of the world, either religion or law that did so highly exalt the public good as the Bible.

—Bacon

THE BOOK

The Bible is a treasure. It contains enough to make us rich for time and eternity. It contains the secret of happy living. It contains the title-deeds of an inheritance incorruptible, and that fadeth not away. It contains the pearl of great price. Nay, in so far as it reveals them as the portion of us sinful worms, it contains the Saviour and the living God Himself.

—James Hamilton

The Book

Benjamin Weiss

Ben Weiss is 94 years young and still going strong. He has served as a high school principal, twenty-five years; president of Christian Educators Fellowship, twenty-six years. He served on the International Board of Youth For Christ and the California Governors committee on education.

It is an authentic record of the human race to live in relation to God. It relates failure and success without favor or hostility.

It is a literary masterpiece of short stories and incidents, poetry and prose. It relates the experiences, aspirations and daily happenings of common folk, kings, servants, and leaders to live and prosper, according to God's will.

It has a unique dynamic authority, usually spoken of as inspired or Divine revelation. The entire book verifies this.

In reading, it produces a wholesome effect. It makes me a more worthy companion, a better citizen, a more effective leader and a more reliable person. The message relates to me personally.

It gives insight about my relation to others; my family, my friends, leaders, the weak, the hurting, and all that compose society. The high motive of love is offered with a test line, "Love your neighbor as yourself."

The common every-day things of life are enhanced. The answer to "what it is all about," included. It presents a divine purpose in history in a person, Jesus Christ. It is for me, for now, for eternity.

The Bible, the Best

Cowley

What can we imagine more proper for the ornaments of wit and learning in the story of Deucalion than in that of Noah? Why will not the actions of Samson afford as plentiful matter as the labours of Hercules? Why is not Jephthah's daughter as good a woman as Iphigenia? And the friendship of David and Jonathan more worthy celebration than that of Theseus and Pirithous? Does not the passage of Moses and the Israelites into the Holy Land yield incomparably more poetic variety than the voyages of Ulysses or AEneas? Are the obsolete, threadbare tales of Thebes and Troy half so stored with great, heroical, and supernatural actions (since verse will needs, find or make such) as the wars of Joshua, of the Judges, of David, and divers others? Can all the transformations of the gods give such copious hints to flourish and expatiate upon as the true miracles of Christ, or of his prophets and apostles? What do I instance in these few particulars? All the books of the Bible are either already most admirable and exalted pieces of poesy, or are the best materials in the world for it.

Robert Hall

The veneration we shall feel for the Bible as the depository of *saving knowledge* will be totally distinct, not only from what we attach to any other book, but from that admiration its other properties inspire; and the variety and antiquity of its history, the light it affords in various researches, its inimitable touches of nature, together with the sublimity and beauty so copiously poured over its pages, will be deemed subsidiary ornaments, the embellishments of the casket which contains the *pearl of great price*.

Great Americans and The Book

"The American nation from its first settlement in Jamestown to this hour is based upon and permeated by the Bible."

—Supreme Court Justice Brewer

"If we abide by the principles taught in the Bible, our country will go on prospering and to prosper; but if we and our posterity neglect its instructions and authority, no man can tell how sudden a catastrophe may overwhelm us and bury our glory in profound obscurity."

—Daniel Webster

"It is impossible to enslave mentally or socially a Bible-reading people. The principles of the Bible are the groundwork of human freedom."

—Horace Greeley

"The Bible is worth all the other books which have ever been printed."

—Patrick Henry

"The Bible is a book in comparison with which all others in my eyes are of minor importance; and which in all my perplexities and distresses has never failed to give me light and strength."

—Robert E. Lee

Columbus and The Bible

"It was the Lord who put into my mind (I could feel His hand upon me) the fact that it would be possible to sail from here to the Indies. All who heard of my project rejected it with laughter, ridiculing me. There is no question that the inspiration was from the Holy Spirit, because He comforted me with rays of marvelous inspiration from the Holy Scriptures. . . ."

Baroness Maria von Trapp and The Bible

"I grew up in Austria and took the Bible for granted, except I didn't read it. It was there, and I was there, but I didn't have any real connection with it.

"I don't remember why, but I do remember how one day when I was in my late twenties, I opened the Bible and was just amazed. I couldn't stop reading. I started in the New Testament, and then went back to the Old, and there I found with growing excitement the answers to all the questions—how it all started, what is the most important thing in life. It is all there.

"It's like a beacon to get your connections from."

"Whereby are given unto us exceeding great and precious promises."

—2 Peter 1:4

Presidents and The Bible

"The meaning of the Bible must be known and understood if it is to make a difference in our lives, and I urge all Americans to read and study the Scriptures. The rewards of such efforts will help preserve our heritage of freedom and signal the message of liberty to people in all lands."

— Ronald Reagan

"I have made it a practice every year for several years to read through the Bible."

— John Adams

"The teachings of the Bible are so interwoven with our whole civic and social life that it would be literally impossible for us to figure what life would be if those teachings are removed."

— Teddy Roosevelt

"So great is my veneration of the Bible that the earlier my children begin to read it the more confident will be my hope that they will prove useful citizens of their country and respectable members of society."

— John Quincy Adams

"America was born a Christian nation. America was born to exemplify that devotion to the elements of righteousness which are derived from the Holy Scriptures."

— Woodrow Wilson

Billy Graham and The Book

The Word of God is the only real authority we have. His Word sheds light on human nature, world problems and human suffering. But beyond that, it clearly reveals the way to God.

The message of the Bible is the message of Jesus Christ who said, "I am the way, the truth, and the life" (John 14:6). It is the story of salvation; the story of your redemption and mine through Christ; the story of life, of peace, of eternity.

Our faith is not dependent upon human knowledge and scientific advance, but upon the unmistakable message of the Word of God.

The Bible has a great tradition and a magnificent heritage. It contains 66 books written over a period of several hundred years by many different men. Yet the message, divinely inspired by the Holy Spirit, is clear throughout. The 66 books become one.

The Bible is old; yet it is ever new. It is the most modern book in the world today. There is a false notion that a book as ancient as the Bible cannot speak to the needs of modern man. Men somehow think that in an age of scientific achievement, when knowledge has increased more in the past 25 years than in all preceding centuries put together, this ancient Book is out of date. But to all who read and love the Bible, it is relevant for our generation.

It is in the Holy Scriptures that we find the answers to life's ultimate questions: Where did I come from? Why am I here? Where am I going? What is the purpose of my existence?

The Bible, the greatest document available for the human race, needs to be opened, read and believed.

"The Lord gave the word."—Psalm 68:11

Wernher Von Braun and The Book

"The raw material of religion is faith. Faith in the written word of the Scriptures and the spoken words of the prophets, of Christ Himself, the apostles and the saints. We love these words because they convey so effectively the time-honored truths that were thus revealed to man throughout the centuries. And St. Peter's Church, by codifying these words, has established the Bible as the most effective bulwark ever built against the erosive effects of time.

"The interpretation of biblical passages has been subject to arguments between wiser men than I for centuries. The fragmentation of the Christian Church is vivid proof that there is no easy answer. I do not want to hurt anyone's feelings by offering a glimpse of my own views on the delicate topic. I find that it helps to bridge the gap between the Bible and modern scientific thought if we remember that the Bible, while it is primarily the revelation of God and His moral law, deals with man as well as God, and that most of the people of whom the Bible speaks suffered from the same human frailties which we experience today. Yes, the very fact that the Bible presents the story of God against the background of people as we all know them is what makes it the best-known book in human history."

All flesh is grass, and all the goodliness thereof is as the flower of the field: the grass withereth, the flower fadeth; because the spirit of the Lord bloweth upon it; surely the people is grass. The grass withereth the flower fadeth, but the word of our God shall stand forever.

—Isaiah xl. 6

The Book and the Books

by Wilbur Smith
Excerpt, Treasury of Books

I trust that the bringing together of these studies, chiefly relating to Biblical subjects, will arouse in many ministers a desire for a more serious, constant study of the Word of God, and of the great books that have been written to help us understand these Divine oracles. And I can also hope that some things set forth here will save many from wasting money and time in the purchase and reading of those superficial works which, however glowing might be their blurbs and advertising, will fade into oblivion before a given year is past. Some of the chapters are not primarily guides to literature, but, occasionally, outlines of some Biblical subject.

In these pages I am only attempting to give some guidance to those who want to read, and who know they should read, but who are bewildered by the large number of books they observe in the bookstores or see advertised in religious journals. Even the Apostle Paul, author of the most profound treatises the Church will ever know, after all those wonderful years of evangelism, in the last days of his life on earth, knowing that at any time he might be called out of the Mamertine Prison to lay down his life for Christ, asked Timothy to bring "the books and the parchments." He never lost his love for reading, and no doubt he never had the time for reading all that he longed to read.

The Scriptures teach us the best way of living, the noblest way of suffering, and the most comfortable way of dying.

—Flavel

A Businessman Looks at the Bible

by W. Maxey Jarman,
Former Chairman, Genesco, Inc.

"I apply these same principles to everything in life, and especially to the Bible. I have read it, studied it, believed it, and applied it in my own life, and I can recommend it to everyone because it is worth the price. I believe it deserves your most careful consideration.

"If you have lived according to man's wisdom, you have a good idea of what it offers. Why not try living according to God by letting the Holy Spirit speak to you through His Book? You will find it offers far more benefits than those I have mentioned. Jesus said that He came that we might have life and have it more abundantly, and perhaps this is the best description of the new life that you will discover. The spiritual rebirth is so far beyond our human understanding that you will begin to know what it means only when you live it, when you feel the embryo within you beginning to grow. Then you will experience a new internal joy, a readiness to meet life's burdens, and a willingness to look toward the future with serenity and assurance."

Theodore Parker

The Bible goes equally to the cottage of the plain man and the palace of the king. It is woven into literature, and it colours the talk of the street. The bark of the merchant cannot sail to sea without it. No ship of war goes to conflict but the Bible is there. It enters men's closets; mingling in all grief and cheerfulness of life.

The Bible: Guide for the Businessman

by: Marion Wade,
Former Chairman, Service Master Company

I've heard of men who admittedly turned their business over to the Lord in the expectation that this was the surest and swiftest road to riches. In effect they were saying: "God is incapable of failure, so now my company should really take off." I wonder how many such men run one of the 15,000 companies that will go out of business this year. The Lord never offered to take over a man's life to such an extent. To each of us He gave a free will, and even the man who has made himself completely dependent on the Lord has to make his own decisions and be responsible for them. But the Lord has provided the basis for right decisions in the Bible and a man can't ask for much more than that.

Often I am asked how to use the Bible for guidance, at least how I use it. There is only one way: to become so familiar with the Bible that thinking in terms of it is part of your nature. The man who has never held a Bible in his hands before would do best to start with the gospels by Matthew, Mark, Luke and John. If he has gone to church at all in his life, he will be somewhat acquainted with what these writers have to say. Even if his knowledge is limited to what he has seen in Bible-based movies or what he reads in newspapers around Easter and Christmas, he will have something to start with.

Darmsteter

Humanity can never deny the Bible in its heart, without the sacrifice of the best that it contains, faith in unity and hope for justice, and without a relapse into the mythology and the "might makes right" of thirty centuries ago.

Booker T. Washington
and The Book

As we watch Booker T. Washington through the eyes of his students and his faculty as they came into relationship with him, the true quality of his greatness is thrown into ever clearer relief. He was great. He was in the truest sense great. We see this, not simply in the titanic achievement of Tuskegee Institute, nor in the world-wide fame that he achieved, but most of all in the quality and creative effect of his personal relationships with the young. The aim and influence of the Superman is to make other men – even other great men – small. The aim and influence of Booker Washington made small men great. He helped the young envenomed Purdues and the frustrated Tom Campbells to cleanse and to free their inner powers that had been dammed up by evil circumstance. When we look for the secret of that kind of greatness we find it again in contrast with the Superman. From Nietzche onward, the hallmark of the Superman has been contempt for the personality of others. Booker Washington's greatness lay in reverence for the personality of the most ragged, illiterate lout. He held this view not because of a vague sentimentalism, but because he saw the germ of life hidden within the rough husk and longed to help it to break through in bud and flower and fruit. And the wellspring of his reverence lay in his constant renewal of it in HIS DAILY READING OF THE BOOK which, on its first page, says that the Eternal Creator breathed the breath of life into man so that he became "a living soul," and on its last page envisages the triumph of His Son who said, "it is not the will of your Father . . . that one of these little ones should perish."

R. G. Lee and The Book

There were not too many books available in Bob's early life. But there were two books which had a greater influence upon him than all others: one of these was a dictionary, the other the Bible.

Bob early recognized the value of words. Having an irresistible urge to become a minister, he wanted to build up a vocabulary. As he became more skilled in the use of words, he developed the habit of trying to use the proper word for each occasion. When he became a minister he became a master of alliteration.

But Lee attributes his ultimate success to his belief in the Word of God. To him the Bible was the Book of all books. Through the years he has been steadfastly loyal to the truths as presented in the Scriptures. He has depended upon the Bible promises and he has obeyed the Bible's commands. The Bible has been proved as God's Word in his own life and by its influence upon others. No critical theories can detract from his own experience with the Word. Lee says today that the Bible is immeasurable, inestimable in value, inerrant in statement, inexhaustive in adequacy, regenerative in power, personal in application, the miracle Book of diversity in unity, of harmony in infinite complexity.

> —from *Robert G. Lee, The Authorized Biography*, by John E. Huss

It is a belief in the Bible, the fruits of deep meditation, which has served me as the guide of my moral and literary life. I have found it a capital safely invested, and richly productive of interest.

> —Goethe

Billy Sunday and The Book

Twenty-two years ago, with the Holy Spirit as my guide I entered the wonderful temple of Christianity. I entered at the portico of Genesis, walked down through the Old Testament art galleries, where pictures of Noah, Abraham, Moses, Joseph, Isaac, Jacob, and Daniel hung on the wall. I passed into the music room of Psalms, where the Spirit swept the key-board of nature until it seemed that every reed and pipe in God's great organ responded to the tuneful harp of David, the sweet singer of Israel. I entered the chamber of Ecclesiastes, where the voice of the preacher was heard; and into the conservatory of Sharon, and the Lily of the Valley's sweet-scented spices filled and perfumed my life. I entered the business office of Proverbs, and then into the observatory room of the Prophets, where I saw telescopes of various sizes, pointed to far off events, but all concentrated upon the bright and morning star.

I entered the audience room of the King of Kings, and caught a vision of His glory from the standpoint of Matthew, Mark, Luke, and John, passed into the Acts of the Apostles, where the Holy Spirit was doing his work in the formation of the infant church. Then into the correspondence room, where sat Paul, Peter, James, and John, penning their epistles. I stepped into the throne room of Revelation, where towered the glittering peaks, and got a vision of the King sitting upon the throne in all His glory, and I cried:

> "All hail the power of Jesus' name,
> Let angels prostrate fall,
> Bring forth the royal diadem,
> And crown him Lord of all"

Vance Havner and The Book

The storehouse of God's Word was never meant for mere scrutiny, not even primarily for study but for sustenance. It is not simply a collection of fine proverbs and noble teachings for men to admire and quote as they might Shakespeare. It is rations for the soul, resources of and for the spirit, treasure for the inner man. Its goods exhibited upon every page are ours, and we have no business merely moving respectfully amongst them and coming away none the richer.

The window-shopper upon the streets often has a very good reason for not buying: he has not the wherewithal. But no believer can say that of God's riches, for the treasure of His Word is without money and without price. Whosoever will may drink freely. Some window-shop because they never have fully realized that the things of the Spirit can be made actual, living realities here and amidst this humdrum, daily round of commonplace duties. Others loaf along, indifferent to their inward poverty, faring scantily when the banquets of God are at their disposal. And some substitute wishful longing for the practical realization of the Christ-life.

The Lord is rich unto all who call upon Him. Let us have done with this idle window-shopping. Let us go into the deep stores of His Word, rummage among its treasures new and old, and come forth from each excursion laden with the bounty in the Book.

The Bible is God's chart for you to steer by, to keep you from the bottom of the sea, and to show you where the harbor is, and how to reach it without running on rocks or bars.

—Henry Ward Beecher

The Right Translation?

by C. S. Lewis

There is no such thing as translating a book into another language once and for all, for a language is a changing thing. If your son is to have clothes it is no good buying him a suit once and for all: he will grow out of it and have to be reclothed.

We ought therefore to welcome all new translations (when they are made by sound scholars) and most certainly those who are approaching the Bible for the first time will be wise not to begin with the Authorised Version – except perhaps for the historical books of the Old Testament where its archaisms suit the saga-like material well enough. Among modern translations those of Dr. Moffatt and Monsignor Knox seem to me particularly good. The present volume concentrates on the epistles and furnishes more help to the beginner: its scope is different. The preliminary abstracts to each letter will be found especially useful, and the reader who has not read the letters before might do well to begin by reading and reflecting on these abstracts at some length before he attempts to tackle the text. It would have saved me a great deal of labour if this book had come into my hands when I first seriously began to try to discover what Christianity was.

– God in the Dock, 1970

"The word of the Lord endureth for ever."
– I Peter 1:25a

Early Translations

Many persons have never reflected on the circumstance that one of the earliest translations of the Scriptures into a vernacular tongue was made by the Church of Rome. The Latin Vulgate was so called from its being in the vulgar — *i.e.*, the popular — language then spoken in Italy and the neighbouring countries: and that version was evidently made on purpose that the Scriptures might be intelligently read by, or read to, the mass of the people. But gradually and imperceptibly Latin was superseded by the languages derived from it, — Italian, Spanish, and French, — while the Scriptures were still left in Latin; and when it was proposed to translate them into modern tongues, this was regarded as a perilous innovation, though it is plain that the real innovation was that which had taken place imperceptibly, since the very object proposed by the Vulgate version was that the Scriptures might *not* be left in an unknown tongue.

—Whately

65.A.24 The Bible is for the government of the people, by the people, and for the people.

*Wycliffe, Preface to first English translation of the Bible, 1384.

We should compare places of Scripture treating of the same point: thus one part of the sacred text could not fail to give light unto another.

—Locke

"Worry Clinic" – March 3, 1984

A daily syndicated column,
by George W. Crane, Ph.D., M.D.

Today's column is my answer to why the Bible is the book that has aided me most as psychologist & psychiatrist.

CASE H-930: Jesus was the greatest Applied Psychologist ever to tread this earth.

Aristotle was the best in the years B.C. and Shakespeare, since the year Christ died.

Note the many innovations, I've put into this column for the past generation and which I derived from the Bible:

(1) Adam's invention of buck-passing re the forbidden fruit and his escape from undue censure by blaming Eve.

(2) God's paying Aaron a compliment and Gideon's probably saving his own life via a compliment, so these led to my creating the "Compliment Club."

(3) Christ's use of the "Reversible Why," to shift the spotlight back on the propounder of dangerous questions, as when the Sanhedrin spies tried to catch Him via their question:

"Is it lawful to pay tribute to Caesar?"

Jesus thus held up a Roman coin; asked whose image was thereon; then told them to render unto Caesar the things that were Caesar's.

(4) Jesus employed the narrative (anecdotal or parable) formula for public speaking, and included humor to make the audiences laugh, as by hyperbole (straining at gnats but swallowing camels).

(5) Jesus advocated our "Free Enterprise" policy, even among preachers, for when John told Him they forbade others from preaching in Christ's name, Jesus countermanded their attempt at religious monopoly.

And He lauded the salesmanship of the men who doubled their talents in the free market. But Christ condemned the communist who was afraid to compete in a free enterprise society.

(6) Jesus also pioneered a national advertising campaign when He sent the 70 Disciples ahead of Him, 2 by 2, to help publicize Christ's forthcoming visits and speeches.

(7) Jesus was doing a poll of public opinions when He probably feigned sleep aboard the ship that His Apostles feared would break apart in the violent storm.

(8) Jesus advocated equal rights for women, gentleness re children, and even forgave His murderers with His last breath on the Cross at Calvary. Did any other deity ever do such?

(9) He died at about A.D. 30, and the first 3 Gospels were written before A.D. 67, about 35 years later, so thousands of eye witnesses were still alive both in Rome and Jerusalem, who could have protested any false statements therein!

(10) More churches, colleges, hospitals, YMCA and youth halls, Red Cross, Salvation Army, plus inspiring music and art, are rooted in the Bible than in ALL other books ever written, so we better use the passport Christ gave us for entrance to Heaven, as stated in Matthew 10:32. Don't delay getting yours!

For the temperature will certainly be pleasanter in Heaven than in Hades!

Also, love there will be gentle and ethereal instead of rapine!

Educators and The Book

William Lyon Phelps

President, Yale University

"I thoroughly believe in a university education for both men and women; but I believe a knowledge of the Bible without a college course is more valuable than a college course without the Bible."

Robert Coles

Professor, Harvard University

My first memories are of my mother reading out of Holy Scripture, from Isaiah or Jeremiah or Amos of the Old Testament, and in the New Testament, Saint Luke, a special favorite of hers, or Saint John to whom she turned when a bit mystical (and she could be so!). She also loved to read to us from Saint Paul's Letters. She loved the messages all right; but she also stressed the beauty of the language – the King James version.

McGeorge Bundy

Former Dean, Harvard University

I don't think you can possibly grow up in an education in which the exposition of the life and the meaning of the life of Jesus is central, and not say that the New Testament is the most important book in your life, however much or little you may have in fact lived by it. It's the most powerful single volume you encounter.

It presents the unattainable standard of decency, or good behavior, or the moral life. Everybody has the problem of living with some kind of notion of what you ought to do, and those are the most powerful notions of 'ought' that I've lived with.

A BOOK I'D LIKE TO SHARE

I use the Scriptures, not as an arsenal to be resorted to only for arms and weapons, but as a matchless temple, where I delight to contemplate the beauty, the symmetry, and the magnificence of the structure, and to increase my awe and excite my devotion to the Deity there preached and adored.

—Boyle

Faith under Fire

by Dr. Ron Herrod
Recommended by: Warren A. Nelson, CLU
Insurance Executive

A book that I have enjoyed tremendously is *Faith under Fire*. It is an inspiration and instruction from the First Epistle of Peter.

Peter wrote I Peter and II Peter to strengthen the early Christians during their testings and trials. They continue to meet a great need for Christians in times like these when we all must demonstrate faith under fire.

Peter reflects on all these aspects of faith:

The basis of your faith (I Peter 1:1–2)
The blessings of your faith (I Peter 1:3–5)
The buffeting of your faith (I Peter 1:6–7)
The birthmarks of your faith (I Peter 1:8–12)
The fruit of your faith (I Peter 1:13–17)
The foundation of your faith (I Peter 1:18–21)
The fellowship of your faith (I Peter 1:22)
The food of your faith (I Peter 1:23–25)

One of the highlights of this book for me is the section entitled "Profit from Suffering." Here, Dr. Herrod states that whether the Christian profits from suffering depends entirely upon the reaction to it. The things that make some people "bitter," make others "better." The same sun that softens the wax hardens the clay.

Many people turn their lemon into lemonade. Others learn to live *above* their circumstances and not *under* them. Phillips Brooks said, "I do not pray for a lighter load but for a stronger back."

The Saving Life of Christ

by Major W. Ian Thomas, D.S.O.
Recommended by: H. Willard Niesen,
Retired—Hamilton Watch Company

The Saving Life of Christ brought to me afresh the importance of looking to Jesus Christ and the Word of God in everything we do. He has told us in the Word —John 15:5, "Without me, ye can do nothing." Thomas says, "How much can we do without him?" Nothing!

It is amazing how busy you can be doing nothing! Did you ever find that out? The flesh—everything that you do apart from Him—profiteth nothing. (John 6:63), and there is always the awful possibility if you do not discover this principle, that you may spend a lifetime in the service of Jesus Christ doing nothing. You would not be the first and you would not be the last— but that, above everything else, we must seek to avoid!

Thomas also points out that there is something which makes Christianity more than a religion and more of an ethic; and more than an idle dream of a sentimental idealist. It is this something which makes it relevant to each one of us right now as a contemporary experience. It is the fact that Christ Himself is the very life content of the Christian faith.

It is for you to be—it is for Him to do! Restfully available to *The Saving Life of Christ,* enjoying the richest measure of the divine presence, a body wholly filled with God Himself, instantly obedient to the heavenly impulse—this is your vocation and this is your victory.

This is what makes the Gospel at once urgent! Mental assent is not enough—a moral choice is imperative! Christ is God's last word to man and God's last word to you, and He demands an answer.

A Spiritual Clinic

by J. Oswald Sanders
Recommended by: Dr. Raymond C. Ortlund,
Pastor, Author, Pasadena California

Here is a dog-eared book. On my shelf and in my life, I love it. I learn from it every time I go to it. Then I go back for more.

This is a book that has helped me face life's realities. Here's a taste —

"overcoming Tension and Strain:" (chapter 1) "Work, per se, is not the real source [of tension] . . . A sense of inadequacy, a haunting consciousness of the lack of spiritual resources and mental acumen . . . is a prolific source of tension. . . . An attitude of anxiety, the habit of worrying over things beyond our power to control, can paralyze the nerve of spiritual endeavor and set up dangerous tension. . . . A wrong attitude to others is fruitful in producing tension. When an inner resentment is harbored, sometimes almost unconsciously, it can work havoc with the nervous system, as will envy, jealousy, ill will, and hatred. . . . Is there a way out of this prison house, a real possibility of deliverance? Is it merely pursuing a mirage to expect God to

'Take from our lives the strain and stress,
And let our ordered lives confess
The beauty of his peace'?

"There is a 'way of escape' which will be found by those who are prepared to be restlessly honest with themselves and God, and who are deeply in earnest in their search for the key. It would seem that the following steps will need to be taken along the road to deliverance.

"Serve the Lord with gladness."

—Psalm 100:2

Character Sketches

by the Institute in Basic Youth Conflicts
Recommended by: G. Frederick Owen,
Educator, Author

The book that has meant the most to our life has been *Character Sketches*. It includes pieces such as:
"True Greatness"

"True greatness requires that we become great in the right areas. This means that we must learn how to be great in faith, great in godly character, great in wisdom, great in self-control, great in patience, great in godliness, great in gentleness, great in love. (II Peter 1:1-10)

"The first step is to become great in faith. 'Without faith it is impossible to please God, for he that cometh to God must believe that He is (God lives) and that He is a rewarder of them that diligently seek Him.' (Hebrews 11:6)

"Every man or woman who achieved a place in God's hall of fame was first and foremost a person of great faith. Faith was not a vague term to them. It was a clear picture of what God intended to do in and through their lives.

"Every Christian must learn to walk by faith and not by sight. This means making decisions that are consistent with the ways of God rather than with the natural inclinations which are contrary to Scripture."

Blessed are they that hear the WORD OF GOD and keep it.
—Luke 11:28

Christianity and History

by Herbert Butterfield
Recommended by: Don Page, Ph.D. historian,
Deputy Director, Department of External Affairs,
Ottawa, Canada

The passage of time into history is something that affects all of us. If we are to profit from the past then it is important that we draw the proper lessons from it. To do this requires that we see it in the light of eternity. What is really important in the light of eternal values? How does God intervene in lives of His people to affect His purpose here on earth?

Herbert Butterfield's *Christianity and History* (London: G. Bell & Sons, 1954), sets the framework for answering such questions. It should be required reading for all those who seek meaning from their past experiences. Butterfield's insights will enlighten all our reading so that we may search out the truth and be better able to profit from it and have a positive impact on the society around us. World events are neither abstract catastrophes nor mundane happenings, but God's revelations that we might draw closer to Him through a better understanding of His divine intervention and inspiration. This book will start the reader thinking in this direction.

"Worship him that made heaven, and earth, and the sea."

—Revelation 14:7

Here's How to Succeed with Your Money

by George M. Bowman
Recommended by: Ralph Palmen, Professional Speaker

An empty feeling in my life was causing me to search for answers. The first place I looked was the church. There I had a personal encounter with God. I decided to turn my life over to Him and let Him control my destiny. To my great relief I found that decision brought real peace to my heart. I had found something real and was a changed person on the inside.

Even though the purpose of my life had changed, I still had some hang-ups and conflicts about money. I was still trying to operate with many of my old habits and attitudes toward money, even though I had changed basic direction of motivation. These attitudes kept me in financial bondage even though I had found spiritual freedom.

I found a book called *Here's How to Succeed with Your Money.*

In his book Mr. Bowman explained how a Christian should think about money. He stated that "money is not the root of all evil. The Bible says the Love of money is the root of all evil." He went on to explain that Christians not only have an opportunity to succeed with their money . . . they have a responsibility to succeed with their money. His practical teaching based on Bible principles helped me develop a workable financial plan that enabled me to find financial freedom that was compatible with my spiritual freedom.

I can surely testify to the power of a book to help transform a person's life.

When Caring Is Not Enough

by David Augsburger
Recommended by: Bob Phillips,
Author, Psychologist, Counselor

I would like to share with you a truly fantastic book entitled *When Caring Is Not Enough*, by David Augsburger. It is subtitled, "Resolving Conflicts Through Fair Fighting."

Just as I am convinced that conflict is a part of life, I am also convinced that I have not been adequately prepared to deal with conflict. I can't remember any courses being offered in school in the area of "How to Deal with Interpersonal Conflict." It seems strange that in education we spend so much time learning facts and so little time in learning how to communicate and get along with others.

In his book, David Augsburger begins to bridge the gap caused by conflict in interpersonal relationships. He gives us valuable tools for dealing with troublesome relationships, whether they are between family members, friends or people we work with.

Augsburger sets forth a thirty-day plan for learning fair-fighting skills. He begins each of the thirty sections by identifying the issue involved and then he shows the reader the negative and positive ways to deal with the issue. He calls the negative methods "fouls" and the positive methods "fair-fighting."

When Caring Is Not Enough is definitely a must book for anyone who wants to grow personally, wants to help others grow, and wants to learn how to effectively deal with interpersonal conflict. I highly recommend this book and all the others written by David Augsburger.

Deeper Experiences of Famous Christians

by James Gilchrist Lawson
Recommended by: Dr. William O. Poe, Pastor
Independence, Missouri

This book challenged and excited me. It is about ordinary men and women who came to a time in their lives when they turned everything over to God: gave Him all the keys to their lives; at which time the Holy Spirit of God took over and used them as instruments to change the world. This book magnifies the Holy Spirit in the lives of men and women.

Contained in this book are the biographies and autobiographies of saints who lived in another generation. These men and women whose names were once household words, such as, John Bunyan, George Mueller, D.L. Moody, John Wesley, and others, had such a life-changing encounter with God that their names are recorded and preserved in history.

These persons came from all walks of life, all types of backgrounds; but the one common denominator that made them outstanding was their deep spiritual experiences. These experiences, (which were real to the individual and cannot be denied) are motivational, because of the possibility of each of us having a deep experience with God. These encounters with God made them giants.

There are twenty-five failure-to-success, natural-to-supernatural stories in this book. In reading the book, one is inspired and motivated to a higher level of living: the principle being, "All things are possible with God."

The Law of Faith

by Norman Grubb
Recommended by: Don Polston,
Author, Pastor, Waterloo, Iowa

This is a book which deals with faith, a natural faculty; elementary faith to advanced faith; full assurance of faith; the swaying battle of faith; speaking the word of faith; and what is clear guidance. I have carried this book for more than 25 years. It is still on my "read often" list.

Grubb states in the chapter, "Full Assurance of Faith," "So the fight of faith sways to and fro. But note carefully that there should be no fight of faith at all! We only fight and struggle because we are still in the infancy of faith; still seeing men as trees walking. A great veil, indeed, is over the eyes of thousands of Christians because they are given to understand that Christianity is ever a struggle and a strife against inward and outward foes. No. He goes on to say, "So the negative is swallowed up by the positive, the evil overcome by the good. By this method, the evil, the visible, the fallen condition, the oppositions of Satan, are disregarded; while all the energies are concentrated on believing, affirming and standing in the victory of Christ. When this is done," he goes on to say, "the other merely disappears from view. It becomes an unreality to us, like a dream. We have passed out of the principle of darkness into the principle of light, and these two cannot know each other."

Norman Grubb's books cross all denominational lines, all theological barriers, and at times, his freedom to come and go from many different standpoints, would irritate the sensitive reader. But those who are bold and daring will find in his books a thrust, an uplift, and insight which will inspire their lives the rest of their lives. His writings will grab you as in the title of his own life story, "Once caught, no escape."

Rees Howells, Intercessor

by Norman Grubb
Recommended by: Dr. Arnold Prater,
Pastor, Evangelist, Author

I am enjoying my wonderful sixties. I have lived in God's arms most of those years and thought I knew a bit about God's depth, but the story of Rees Howells left me in awe. For I realized I had never even come close to the depths of God that this man knew.

Every Christian should be an intercessor, but some are called to be intercessors. Few have ever had hold of God as did Rees Howells, the Welsh coal miner who founded the Bible College of Wales.

One young Christian asked him how he knew God's voice, to which Rees answered, "Can't you tell your mother's voice from any other?" "Yes, of course," said the young man. "Well, I know His voice just like that," Rees said.

He believed that God's law of intercession meant only insofar as we ourselves become willing to assume the conditions of others, spiritually, and if needs be, physically, can we intercede for others. Even taking their place in death, if need be.

Once he prayed for a man who was the father of ten children and who was given up to die. Rees interceded with God, citing the need for a breadwinner for the family. Healing came only after Rees Howells became completely willing to give up his work and take over the support of the family himself.

He reached such depths of intercession that finally, in almost every case in which he prayed intercessorily, the Holy Spirit revealed to him what the answer would be.

If you want the very foundations of your prayer life completely rebuilt, read this magnificent story. I know I'll never pray the same!

Great Evangelists & Books

John Wesley

The practical books most read by him at this period, which was probably employed as a course of preparation for holy orders were, *The Christian's Pattern,* by Thomas à Kempis; and Bishop Taylor's *Rules of Holy Living and Dying,* and his correspondence with his parents respecting these authors, shows how carefully he was weighing their merits, and investigating their meaning, as regarding them in the light of spiritual instructors.

—Richard Watson, 1835

George Whitefield

George Whitefield read voraciously. In his quest for a closer relationship with Christ, he was led to an obscure, slim volume, **The Life of God in the Soul of Man,** by a forgotten Scot named Henry Scougal. Whitefield was non-plused to discover that all of the good things which he had been doing to earn God's favor were of no account. What he needed, he learned, was to have Christ formed within him; in short, he needed to be "born again."

The Authority of the Believer

by Kenneth E. Hagin
Recommended by: Frederick K.C. Price
Pastor, Inglewood, CA

One of the many books which blessed me and was instrumental in my Christian walk was a book entitled, *The Authority of the Believer* by Kenneth E. Hagin.

The reason this book was so meaningful to me was because it brought into focus an aspect of the Gospel that I had never seen nor ever heard presented to the Body of Christ. Traditionally, the Church has left us Christians with the concept that we were to struggle in this life spiritually, physically and financially because we would reap the benefits of the Christian life when we get to Heaven.

So this life was just to be a holding pattern until we get to Heaven, and *The Authority of the Believer* pointed out to me in a clear, simple and direct way that the traditional idea of the "struggling Christian" was a fallacy and that God wants His children, Christians, to be victorious in this life, spiritually, physically and financially. The concept of the book changed my life forever. It taught me that I could be a winner and not a loser, and all of the concepts in the book are drawn from the Bible, a book that is basically unknown by both clergy and laity.

"I was glad when they said unto me, Let us go into the house of the Lord."
                                                    —Psalm 122:1

The Greatest Thing in the World

by Henry Drummond
Recommended by: Nelson Price, Pastor,
Marietta Georgia

It was near midnight when I retired to the Lincoln Bedroom. Having just finished the assignment for the day given me by the President, I was too exuberant to sleep. Having noticed a book on the desk in the Queen's Bedroom just across the hall of the living quarters in the White House, I quietly crossed over and sat for a while to re-read a book which years earlier had helped transform my life. It was Henry Drummond's, *The Greatest Thing in the World.*

In it, he writes of the "summum bonum," the supreme good, in a refreshing and challenging way. It is a treatise on one of the most needed things in the world today. It deals with the most misunderstood word in the English language. The thing, the word, is love.

When understood, love is seen not as a feeling, an abstract, or an ideology, but as an action. It is behavior. A certain kind of behavior well defined by Drummond.

For a better understanding of proper and productive behavior, this book forms a scaffold on which to build. When the precepts propagated therein are employed, it will change your life and positively impact others throughout.

I returned to the Lincoln Bedroom thinking, "That is a message fit for a queen – or a president, as well as for me."

"Thou hast put gladness in my heart."
—Psalm 4:7

Elemental Theology

by Emery Bancroft
Recommended by: Dr. John W. Rawlings,
Pastor, Cincinnati, Ohio

When I started my ministry full time, one of my seminary professors suggested that every young preacher should memorize a book on theology, Bancroft's *Elemental Theology.*

I bought the book, and began immediately an intensive study of this great writer's position on the subject of the nature of God, His attributes, His identification with man, His acts in creation, the substitutionary death of Christ upon the cross, His promise to return again to this earth, and what is termed the doctrine of last things or the doctrine of eschatology.

I was so intrigued and captured by the fairness of the writer, his method of outlining, his way of emphasizing a profound truth in a practical way, that I decided to memorize the book, and I did.

After looking across almost five decades of Christian service, I can say with deep conviction, this book has anchored my beliefs. I knew them prior to that. I knew what I believed, but in his concise, practical way of defining these truths, he helped me to put doctrine in perspective. It has been a source and tower of strength to me ever since.

Someone has said that a man is known by what he believes, because it is about that, that he expresses himself. If he is unsure of his doctrinal stand when it comes to truth, inspiration, and the battles that arise so constantly in the ministry, he must have something that will help him to be anchored to the Book, so that he will not preach his doubts, but preach, "thus saith the Lord."

I can say this book helped to anchor, direct and challenge me in the Christian faith.

Jim Rayburn and a Book

Founder of Young Life

Home in Clifton was a decrepit old wooden structure with no luxuries except for a small library. One night, while Max was at the movie theater, Jim discovered an old coverless copy of a book that would change his life. Called *He that Is Spiritual,* it was by Lewis Sperry Chafer, president of a seminary in Dallas, Texas. The book was about the Holy Spirit, grace, and salvation. Jim had never understood these subjects as Chafer presented them.

"How misleading is the theory," Chafer wrote, "that to be spiritual one must abandon play, diversion, and helpful amusement. Such a conception is born of a morbid human conscience. It is foreign to the Word of God. It is a device of Satan to make the blessings of God seem abhorrent to people who are overflowing with physical life and energy. There are many who in blindness are emphasizing negatives, giving the impression that spirituality is opposed to joy, liberty, and naturalness of expression in thought and life in the Spirit. True spirituality is not a pious pose. It is not a 'Thou shalt not,' it is a 'Thou shalt.' We cannot be normal physically, mentally, or spiritually if we neglect this vital factor in human life. God has provided that our joy shall be full."

Dr. Chafer's book had spoken straight to Jim's heart, and he opened his heart's door to receive the risen Christ. Jim had stepped into the realm of the spirit one dark and quiet night as he read by the light of a candle, and as the candle's light faded away in the dawn of a new day, Jim knew the great Seeker had found him.

—Jim Rayburn III

Adventure of Living

by Paul Tournier
Recommended by: C.W. Reaves,
President, Creative Consultants, Inc.

My brother, Lloyd, was aware of a big career decision I was about to make when he gave me a book which changed my life.

Paul Tournier's *Adventure of Living* tells us that the real adventure in life lies in the pursuit of our goals. Big career decisions lead to big adventures which control the direction of our life and the quality of the adventure.

The most important problem with which we now have to deal is that of the adventure. Periodic renewal is necessary because goals and objectives (adventures) are always running out. Always sooner than we think.

Every age is an adventure. Every life is an adventure. Every adventure has its own individuality, which cannot be mixed with any other. As time rolls on, adventure succeeds adventure, but each remains distinct – one from another.

Basically the quality of the adventure is the personal commitment to the decision. Once the full commitment is made, we are no longer free to stop. Total commitment means to bring each adventure to a conclusion. We must decide if a commitment decision will result in a duty to perform, or a new adventure. God guides us, despite our uncertainties and vagueness; even through our failings and mistakes.

Your new adventure is starting as you read these few thoughts. The Holy Spirit is always calling us to look forward – not back.

Pilgrim's Progress

by John Bunyan
Recommended by: Ernest Reisinger,
Pastor, Author, Pompano Beach, Florida

Pilgrim's Progress has influenced my life and helped me understand myself and people more than any other book, except the Bible.

The children read it for the story; the students for its literature value; the theologians read it for its theology.

Bunyan had better insight into the human heart than modern psychology; namely, because he did not study man apart from his Creator and apart from his deep inward problem.

We must not miss one of Bunyan's chief characters, Mr. Fearing. Dr. Alexander Whyte said of him, "For humor, for pathos, for tenderness, for acute and sympathetic insight at once into nature and grace, for absolutely artless literary skill, and for the sweetest, most musical, and most exquisite English, show me another passage in our whole literature to compare with John Bunyan's portrait of Mr. Fearing. You cannot do it. I defy you to do it. Spenser, who, like John Bunyan, wrote an elaborate allegory, says: It is not in me. Take all Mr. Fearing's features together, and even Shakespeare himself has no such heart-touching and heart-comforting character."

The last reason it is so relevant is because we must all cross the "River that has no bridge" – here Bunyan is at his best.

I do not believe any single person has ever plumbed the depth of *Pilgrim's Progress*.

The Agony and the Ecstasy

by Irving Stone
Recommended by: Naomi Rhode, CPAE
Professional Speaker

I was greatly impressed by Irving Stone's dedication to excellence in his five year research of Michelangelo's life and times; impressed with the accuracy and complexity of his product, *The Agony and the Ecstasy;* impressed and, yes, overwhelmed by the life of Michaelangelo – a long life, an unselfish life, a life of an artist who strove for immaculate perfection in the portrayal of his subjects in various media. His obsession carried him into locked mortuaries where the scientists had not even dared to trespass. Here he studied late at night, the anatomy of the human body so as to be able to correctly portray the meaning of muscles and bone in the human anatomy. He was daring beyond his time, he was creative and single minded, he had visions to share with the world, and he accomplished his task.

The most moving excerpt is the story, of his fashioning of the David statue. Many had tackled this assignment ahead of him, using the post-Goliath victory as the focal point for their David and his portrayed attitude. But not Michelangelo! He chose to create the David holding the stone in his hand before the attack on Goliath. A very young lad, seemingly powerless against a giant Goliath, but with a total assurance of victory in his face and stature because he knew Who was impowering and directing his throw. Amazing!

I invite you to read or reread this powerful book, perhaps in a new light, as you ask yourself the question, "Have I won the battle before I throw the stone, because I know Who's directing its path?" Life then is truly directed towards victory and its realization will shine on our faces before the battles begin.

The Light and the Glory

by Peter Marshall and David Manuel
Recommended by: Marvin G. Rickard, Pastor
Los Gatos, California

No book more clearly and reasonably defines the unique blessings of God on America than this one. Its title is taken from a letter John Adams wrote his wife Abigail, saying, "I am well aware of the toil and blood and treasure that it will cost us to maintain this Declaration and support and defend these States. Yet through all the gloom I can see rays of ravishing light and glory."

The authors make an intriguing study to show that Columbus was guided by God to America because of his prayers and faith and that those with faith who followed made a covenant with God that He bless and protect the land in direct proportion to their obedience to Him.

They answer the question, "Does God intervene on behalf of nations whose citizens pray and trust in Him?," with story after fascinating story from our past.

Today's national drift into secular humanism is seen in a new light as one reads *The Light and The Glory.* Blessings, prosperity, and protection of the nation are the direct result of faith in God and obedience by the people. Chaos, trouble, tragedy, and disintegration follow on the heels of declining personal faith.

No one will be quite the same after reading *The Light and the Glory.*

"Let us do good unto all men."
—Galatians 6:10

Rees Howells: Intercessor

by Norman Grubb
Recommended by: Pat Robertson, Pres.
Christian Broadcasting Network, Inc.

There are many books that have influenced my life. This is one of the many examples of prayer life of Rees Howells.

On June 6, the day of the opening of the Second Front, Mr. Howells read with great approval General Eisenhower's Order of the Day to the assault troops, in which he said, "The hopes and prayers of liberty-loving people everywhere march with you . . . let us all beseech the blessing of Almighty God upon this great and noble undertaking." In the meeting Mr. Howells said: "If there is going to be a Day of Prayer, it ought to be a day of victory and moving God." And in his own prayer at the end of that meeting, thinking of the assault troops already landing in Normandy, he prayed, "If You hadn't intervened at Dunkirk, not one of us would be here today. So lay a burden on us, don't allow us to be slack. If Hitler had won, Christianity, civilization and freedom would have gone. Oh Lord, protect and keep our men! Don't allow us to pray any differently from what we would if we were on the front line. We do believe the end of this will be victory."

Finally, on July 8, he said: "I don't think there is anything to compare with the night we invaded Normandy. We said that God was going before our men, and it wasn't going to be like Dunkirk. The Daily Telegraph reported that it was only that night the U-Boats did not patrol the channel. The way we went over to Normandy was beyond imagination—4,000 ships and 11,000 planes—and they never met a single ship or plane of the enemy! God said, 'I am going over and there won't be a set-back': and although, while I am preaching, there is a big battle on, I go back to His word that there will be no reverses."

The Pursuit of God

by A.W. Tozer
Recommended by: Frank D. Robinson, Jr.,
Wendt Food Brokers

The Pursuit of God helped start me on a path of conscious personal awareness of God. Seeking to know Him better became my primary goal. It has added balance and a new dimension of greater purpose to my life.

As each man seeks to know God better, his focus on the things of the Spirit will take shape in his mind, will, and emotion. Purpose, fulfillment, and reward will not depend on things, circumstances, people, or what people have, think, or say.

In the chapter on "Restoring the Creator-Creature Relation," Tozer says:

"Let the seeking man reach a place where life and lips join to say continually 'Be thou exalted,' and a thousand minor problems will be solved at once. His Christian life ceases to be the complicated thing it had been before, and becomes the very essence of simplicity. By the exercise of his will he has set his course, and on that course he will stay, as if guided by an automatic pilot. If blown off course for a moment by some adverse wind, he will surely return again as by a secret bent of the soul. The hidden motions of the Spirit are working in his favor, and 'the stars in their courses' fight for him. He has met his life problem at its center, and everything else must follow along."

"Do that which is right and good."
—Deuteronomy 6:18

Decision Making and the Will of God

by Garry Friesen
Recommended by Doug Ross, Writer, Consultant

After our home was gutted by fire on Christmas Eve of 1981, my wife and I became fully aware of the truth of scripture – that rain does indeed fall on both the just and the unjust. As we rebuilt our home during the next few months, I realized that God didn't cause the fire – or wasn't trying to teach us anything because of it – but I did know He was there with us all the time. God doesn't cause tragedies but rather knocks gently and loves thoroughly.

In Garry Friesen's book, the Christian is reminded of a "biblical alternative to the traditional view." Some of us hold as truth the traditional view that God has a specific plan of our lives, and it's up to us to find it.

God does guide His children. The question is, "How does He guide?"

This book does an excellent job of summarizing traditional views concerning the will of God. In Part II of the book, these views are discussed according to the meaning of Scripture verses that we normally use to justify our everyday actions.

Part III gets down to the real business of how we can determine the will of God for our lives and this the author calls, "The Way of Wisdom."

God mediates His wisdom to us through His Word, our personal research, wise counselors and the applied lessons of life.

The final section of the book is titled, "Deciding the Big Ones." Here you're given volumes of insight into such subjects as "Singleness, Marriage and Wisdom," "The Ministry and Wisdom," "Wisdom When Christians Differ" and "Weaker Brothers, Pharisees and Servants."

Decision Making and the Will of God will benefit you a great deal – no matter where and when the rain falls.

The Christian's Secret of a Happy Life

by Hannah Whitall Smith
Recommended by: James Rudisill,
Past Pres., Printing Industry of America
and Rudisill Printing Company

"Our souls were made to live in this upper atmosphere, and we stifle and choke on any lower level. Our eyes were made to look off from these heavenly heights, and our vision is distorted by any lower gazing. It is a great blessing, therefore, that our loving Father in heaven has mercifully arranged all the discipline of our lives with a view to teaching us to fly.

"In Deuteronomy we have a picture of how this teaching is done: 'As an eagle stirreth up her nest, fluttereth over her young, spreadeth abroad her wings, taketh them, beareth them on her wings: so the Lord alone did lead him, and there was no strange god with him.'

"The mother eagle teaches her little ones to fly by making their nest so uncomfortable that they are forced to leave it and commit themselves to the unknown world of air outside. And just so does our God to us. He stirs up our comfortable nests, and pushes us over the edge of them, and we are forced to use our wings to save ourselves from fatal falling. Read your trials in this light, and see if you cannot begin to get a glimpse of their meaning. Your wings are being developed."

"My sheep hear my voice, and I know them, and they follow me."
—John 10:27

The Pursuit of Holiness

by Jerry Bridges
Recommended by: Jim Ryan,
Football Player, Denver Broncos

This book dealt with sin in a very practical way. I discovered that a "holy" and "pure" life is possible in today's world.

"Our first problem is that *our attitude toward sin is more self-centered than God-centered*. We are more concerned about our own 'victory' over sin than we are about the fact that our sins grieve the heart of God. We cannot tolerate failure in our struggle with sin chiefly because we are success-oriented, not because we know it is offensive to God.

"W. S. Plumer said, 'We never see sin aright until we see it as against God. . . . All sin is against God in this sense: that it is His law that is broken, His authority that is despised, His government that is set at naught. . . . Pharoah and Balaam, Saul and Judas each said, 'I have sinned'; but the returning prodigal said, 'I have sinned *against heaven* and before thee'; and David said, 'Against Thee, Thee only have I sinned.'

"God wants us to walk in *obedience*—not victory. Obedience is oriented toward God; victory is oriented toward self. This may seem to be merely splitting hairs over semantics, but there is a subtle, self-centered attitude at the root of many of our difficulties with sin. Until we face this attitude and deal with it we will not consistently walk in holiness."

Pittsburgh Steelers – Bible Study Fellowship

Lectures To My Students, by Charles Haddon Spurgeon
Recommended by: Hollis Hoff, Bible Study Leader

How Come Its Taking Me So Long To Get Better, by Lane Adams
Recommended by: Mike Webster, All Pro

Three Steps Forward, by Chuck Swindoll
Recommended by: John Stallworth, All Pro

Seasons of Life, by Chuck Swindoll
Recommended by: Donnie Shell, All Pro

Miraculous Gifts, by Thomas Edgar
Recommended by: Tony Dungy, Defensive Coordinator

Paul Bunyan, by Esther Shephard
Recommended by: Terry Long, Offensive Lineman

The Lazarus Effect, by Frank Herbert & Bill Ransom
Recommended by: Edmund Nelson, Defensive Tackle

A Hunters Fireside Book, by Gene Hill
Recommended by: Weegie Thompson, Wide Receiver

Treasure Island, by Robert L. Stevenson
Recommended by: Scott Campbell, Quarterback

Sand Country Almanac, by Aldo Leopold
Recommended by: Loren Toews, 11 year Line Backer

Thirty-Nine Steps, by John Buchan
Recommended by: Gary Anderson, Kicker

Frankenstein, by Mary Shelley
Recommended by: Craig Colquitt

Instant Replay, by Jery Kramer
Recommended by: Craig Wolfley, Offensive Guard

Greatest Success in the World, by Og Mandino
Recommended by: Kirk McJunkin

Encourage Me

by Charles Swindoll
Recommended by: Ron Sams,
Football Player, Minnesota Vikings

"You can talk all you want about diamonds or dinosaur teeth or marble-sized pearls. Sure they are rare. Sure they're tough to find. You've got to tunnel under mountains, excavate ancient lakebeds, or dive to murky depths in mysterious lagoons.

"But I submit that encouragement – genuine, warmhearted, Christ-inspired encouragement – is an even more precious commodity than these. And infinitely more valuable.

"Encouragement is awesome. Think about it: It has the capacity to lift a man's or woman's shoulders. To spark the flicker of a smile on the face of a discouraged child. To breathe fresh fire into the fading embers of a smoldering dream. To actually change the course of another human being's day . . . or week . . . or life.

"That, my friend, is no small thing. But it doesn't stop there. Consistent, timely encouragement has the staggering magnetic power to draw an immortal soul to the God of hope. The One whose name is Wonderful Counselor.

"Is it easy? Not on your life. It takes courage, tough-minded courage, to trust God, to believe in ourselves, and to reach a hand to others. But what a beautiful way to live."

Mission Directors

Romans Verse by Verse

by William R. Newell
Recommended by: Harry Saulnier,
Director, Pacific Garden Mission, Chicago

This book meant a great deal to me because Mr. Newell is so straight on the gospel.

The Crises of the Christ

by G. Campbell Morgan
Recommended by: Sherburn Hill,
Director, Bethesda Mission, Harrisburg, Pa.

Next to the Bible, the book that meant the most to me was *The Crises of the Christ*. I was a new Christian, on business in Los Angeles, and the book was a rewarding grounding in the reality of Christ.

Management for the Christian Leader

Recommended by: Randall Tabor,
Executive Director, Schenectady City Mission

Making of a Man of God

by Alan Redpath
Recommended by: Dick McMillen, Director
Water Street Rescue Mission, Lancaster, PA

The Green Letters:
Principals of Spiritual Growth

by Miles Stanford
Recommended by: Luther Scarborough, Jr.,
Insurance Executive, Million Dollar Round Table

In thinking of a book that has made a significant impact on my life, I would select *Principals of Spiritual Growth* by Miles Stanford. The brief chapters can be gone back over and over. The name itself is meaningful. "Principles" are always valuable. "Growth" is challenging. The book was originally written under the title, *The Green Letters*.

Stanford in the first chapter suggests faith must be based upon certainty. Faith is not a force for which we strive. Just believe hard enough, and it will come to pass. Romans 10:17 tells us faith comes by hearing and hearing by the Word of God. Some of the chapters which I felt were super were: "Time," "Acceptance," "Purpose," "Complete in Him," etc. Powerful principles of a growing life are expressed and expounded upon. I read one time that "it takes a live fish to swim up stream, any old log can float down."

Principals of Spiritual Growth is not a book you finish and forget. I didn't even understand some chapters the first time. We can go back to it and be motivated to think and meditate on spiritual growth. Not only can we go back; but we want to go back. The "Identification" chapter shares real truths that slowly begin to sink in to the learner. Put this book in your library, read it, study it, and share it.

Reading good books is a joy. I look forward to more books. We fully expect to find greater truths in the future. Still, from time to time, I'll want to go back to the *Principals of Spiritual Growth*.

Revival Lectures

by Charles G. Finney
Recommended by: Gerald Schelling,
Pastor, Evangelist, Henry, Virginia

Revival Lectures by Charles G. Finney has been a great influence on my life. Following are some quotes from this book:

"Without a revival, they will grow harder and harder under preaching, and will experience a more horrible damnation than they would if they had never heard the Gospel."

"If we do not go forward, we must go back. Things cannot remain as they are. If the church do not come up, if we do not have a more powerful revival than we have had, very soon we will have none at all. We have had such a great revival, that now small revivals do not interest the public mind. You must act as individuals. Do your own duty. You have a responsibility. Repent quickly. Do not wait till another year. Who but God knows what will be the state of these churches, if things go on another year without a great and general revival. . . .?"

"It is common, when things get all wrong in the church, for each individual to find fault with the church, and with his brethren, and overlook his own share of the blame. Do not let anyone spend his time in finding fault with that abstract thing, 'The church.' But as individual members of the church of Christ, let each one act, and act right, and get down in the dust, and never speak proudly, or censoriously. Go forward. Who would leave such a work, and go to writing letters, and go down into the plain of Ono, and see if all these petty disputes cannot be adjusted, and let the work cease. Let us mind our work, and let the Lord take care of the rest. Do our duty, and leave the issue to God."

The Ultimate Power

by Dave Grant
Recommended by: Dick Semaan, CPAE,
Certified Professional Speaker

I have always been fascinated by the concept of love. I have marvelled at the way God loves people . . . and the way people love each other. I have come to believe that love is the most powerful force in the world today.

That is why Dave Grant's classic book, *The Ultimate Power*, has had such a dynamic impact on my life. His book is subtitled, How To Be a Great Lover of People, and it explores a simple premise . . . IF WE REALLY WANT TO BE HAPPY AND SUCCESSFUL IN THIS WORLD WE MUST LEARN TO UNLEASH THE GREAT POWER OF LOVE IN OUR LIVES!

The following quotations are taken at random and span the entire book.

"A truly GREAT lover is one who loves. To LOVE great is to LIVE great. We cannot live any better than we love. Therefore, love is the KEY to successful living."

"The TRUE success of our lives will not be judged by those who admire US for OUR accomplishments, but by those who attribute THEIR wholeness to OUR loving them, by those who have seen THEIR true beauty and worth in OUR eyes. That's the MEASURE of a GREAT lover."

"Sometimes we want to love someone unconditionally and we find it difficult. But our difficulty has LITTLE to do with the other person. It has a LOT to do with US. We are either LOVING or we are UN-LOVING!"

The Tragic Sense of Life

by Unamuno
Recommended by: Sam Shoemaker,
Pastor and Author

Have you read that remarkable book called *The Tragic Sense of Life* (which is anything but tragic) by Unamuno? There is a poignant sentence in it which goes. "Those who deny God deny Him because of their despair at not finding Him." I am convinced that is profoundly true, psychologically and spiritually. Now what are the ways by which people can reasonably and experimentally break out of the circle of skepticism and unbelief?

The first step is admit that you would like to believe. You can look in any direction you like, and you will, see people in whose lives faith is providing adventure, purpose, courage, integration, or an increase of sheer vitality. You will also, if you look closely enough, see people in whose lives unbelief produces aimlessness, drift, fear, dissipation of energy, and a contraction of natural powers. . . .

I quote Unamuno again, "To believe in God is, in the first instance, to wish that there may be a God, to be unable to live without Him." Whence comes this intense desire for faith? When desire for human hunger sweeps us, we find therein food to satisfy us. When desire for human love comes over us, we find there is such a thing in the world as human love which meets our needs. But why should we be born with this equally intense hunger for faith, unless there were something in this universe to correspond to it, to meet and satisfy it?

—Extraordinary Living for
Ordinary Man, Sam Shoemaker

Professional Baseball

None Dare Call It Treason

by John A. Stormer
Recommended by: Eric Show,
Pitcher, San Diego Padres

There are many books besides the Bible which have had a tremendous impact on my life, but I am selecting a rather obscure and, I believe, suppressed, and unpopular book entitled *None Dare Call It Treason*, by John A. Stormer.

A highly fact-filled and documented book, *None Dare Call It Treason* has, perhaps more than any other book in recent memory, alarmed and enlightened me significantly to the danger that international communism poses to the Christian and free world. The fact that the book itself has remained relatively unknown in spite of its unquestionable documentation is itself, I believe, an indictment of the conspiracy it uncovers. It would certainly be rewarding reading to any open-minded and honest person.

The Pursuit of God

by A. W. Tozer
Recommended by: Frank Tanana,
California Angels

"*The Pursuit of God* will embrace the labor of bringing our total personality into conformity to His. And this not judicially, but actually I do not here refer to the act of justification by faith in Christ. I speak of a voluntary exalting of God to His proper station over us and a willing surrender of our whole being to the place of worshipful submission which the Creator-creature circumstance makes proper."

The Master Plan of Evangelism

by Dr. Robert Coleman
Recommended by: Earl Shultz, V.P.
Youth For Christ, Outreach

Next to the Bible, the book that has impacted me most is *The Master Plan of Evangelism*. When I first read the book it seemed as if the eight principles that Dr. Coleman had outlined should have been obvious to us all. However, it took this man of God to bring them into focus for me. Once discovered, I learned that the principles were easily grasped, relatively easily taught and relatively easily implemented. They are the principles of our Lord Jesus Christ, and should be our principles. The implementation of them will significantly impact our ability to lead, to disciple and ultimately to evangelize.

The following is the Master's plan of evangelism:

1. Selection
2. Association
3. Consecration
4. Impartation
5. Demonstration
6. Delegation
7. Supervision
8. Reproduction

MEN WERE HIS METHOD
HE REQUIRED OBEDIENCE
HE SHOWED THEM HOW TO LIVE
HE EXPECTED RESULTS

What the Bible Teaches

by R. A. Torrey
Recommended by: Vern Sir Louis,
Insurance Executive

What the Bible Teaches was and still is my favorite book. In reviewing it, I would like to point out several reasons for my coming to this conclusion. Although I had been raised in a Christian home and attended a Bible preaching church, it was not until I accepted Jesus Christ as Saviour at age twenty-four that the Bible became of real interest to me. As I began to search for help in how to study the Bible, a friend suggested that if anyone really wants to know about life from a Biblical viewpoint, the book, *What the Bible Teaches*, would be of great help.

I purchased a copy at a local Christian bookstore and after reading only a few pages, was impressed very much with how the Bible has all the answers to whatever questions may surface in the complex world we live in. This book has been a great help to me for the following reasons:

1). What the Bible really teaches is stated in simple terms, with the emphasis on the authority of the Scriptures.

2). It challenges us to depend on God's Word as the final guide on how to live in our complex world.

"Study to show thyself approved unto God."
— II Timothy 2:15

Life of David Brainerd

Recommended by: Oswald J. Smith,
Pastor, Missionary, Toronto, Canada

"So greatly was I influenced by the life of David Brainerd in the early years of my ministry that I named my youngest son after him.

"When I was but eighteen years of age, I found myself 3,000 miles from home, a missionary to the Indians. No wonder I love Brainerd!

"Brainerd, it was, who taught me to fast and pray. I learned that greater things could be wrought by daily contact with God than by preaching.

"When I feel myself growing cold I turn to Brainerd and he always warms my heart. No man ever had a greater passion for souls. To live wholly for God was his one great aim and ambition.

"His missionary challenge, as stated in his letter to his brother, Israel, will ever ring in my ears: "I declare, now I am dying, I would not have spent my life otherwise for the whole world."

"Although Brainerd did his work more than two hundred years ago, he has a message for today. There is nothing we need more than a fresh manifestation of the power of God. Brainerd shows us how it may be obtained."

The harvest truly is great, but the labourers are few: Pray ye therefore the Lord of the harvest, that He would send forth labourers into His harvest.

—Luke 10:2

A Man of the Word

by Jill Morgan
Recommended by: Wilbur M. Smith,
Author, Bible Teacher

"The greatest living expositor of the Scriptures"—
this is the sweeping designation of Dr. G. Campbell
Morgan in the remarkable biography of him, *A Man of
the Word*, by Jill Morgan, the wife of the oldest living
son of Dr. Morgan, the Rev. Frank Crossley Morgan,
of Taft, Texas.

The statement is not in the slightest an exaggera-
tion.

Mrs. Morgan has done a magnificent piece of work.
She has made Dr. Morgan alive, as his earlier biogra-
phers did not. She has had the assistance of all the
members of the family, but she herself has great ability in writing.

My own opinion is that this is the most important
biography of an evangelical minister and laborer in
the Word of God that has appeared since G. F. Barbour
gave us, in 1924, his monumental life of Alexander
Whyte. I wish that I could persuade every Bible-lov-
ing minister in the Western world to read this book
through, behind a locked door, alone with God, as
Campbell Morgan stayed behind a locked door with
the Lord, and the Word of God, every weekday morning, from eight to one, year after year. The fundamental reason for the shameful weakness and barrenness
of much modern preaching is transparently clear
when one discovers the reasons for the power of the
ministry of Campbell Morgan as he labored in the
Word of God, bringing forth things new and old.

"Be still, and know that I am God."
                                        —*Psalm 46:10*

The Sermons of Jonathan Edwards

Recommended by: Dr. R. C. Sproul,
President, Ligonier Valley Study Center

The reason I choose this book is that it focuses on the sweetness of Christ, the Majesty of God, and the centrality of Grace in the Christian life. It is vivid, intense and powerful in its imagery and is able to lift the soul and stir the mind.

"Thus there is a difference between having an opinion that God is holy and gracious, and having a sense of the loveliness and beauty of that holiness and grace. There is a difference between having a rational judgment that honey is sweet and having a sense of its sweetness. A man may have the former that knows not how honey tastes; but a man can not have the latter unless he has an idea of the taste of honey in his mind. So there is a difference between believing that a person is beautiful and having a sense of his beauty. The former may be obtained by hearsay, but the latter only by seeing the countenance. There is a wide difference between mere speculative rational judging anything to be excellent, and having a sense of its sweetness and beauty. The former rests only in the head, speculation only is concerned in it, but the heart is concerned in the latter. When the heart is sensible of the beauty and amiableness of a thing, it necessarily feels pleasure in the apprehension. It is implied in a person's being heartily sensible of the loveliness of a thing, that the idea of it is sweet and pleasant to his soul; which is a far different thing from having a rational opinion that it is excellent."

Christian Principles in Business

by J. C. Penney
Recommended by: James D. Staggs, CEO,
Friendly Ice Cream Corporation

After searching back through my reading experiences, I believe I have gained quite a lot from the many different writings of Peter Drucker, but I think the most positive influence on me very early in my business life was a series of essays written by J. C. Penney concerning key management responsibilities. The title is particularly meaningful because he called it *Christian Principles in Business*, and that is pretty much the tone in which his teachings were cast.

"Wise men do not light a candle and place it under a bushel. Life's greatest benefactions – intelligence, liberty, religion – are for dissemination. There can be no moral justification for withholding the benefits that result from a wise distribution of knowledge.

'Liberty, that one priceless boon for which all men yearn, thrives only in the light. It must be proclaimed and practiced to be enjoyed and appreciated by all.

"Religion was never intended for self-gratification. It must be turned loose upon the world, and the more unconsciously that loosening process takes place, the more beneficial its results.

"Christ declared that He was the Light of the world. Religion must scatter that Light or fail in the accomplishment of its supreme mission."

"Learn to do well." – Isaiah 1:17

The Transformation of the Inner Man

by John and Paula Sandford
Recommended by: Dr. Charles Stanley,
Pastor, Author, Atlanta, Georgia

"This book is not designed to be an essay, nor is it an intellectual exercise. It is not written to act as a purely impersonal, objective teaching device, but to involve the reader's heart. Reading is intended to be experiential, not detached. It may be slow reading. No one should feel guilty if he cannot get through much of it at a time. Many will have to put the book down and ponder awhile. It may require many return readings.

"The end of transformation is not a few scattered individuals who shine as sparks running through the stubble (Isa. 47:14). It is an army of fire blazing a pathway of mercy. No one is fully transformed who does not yet know himself to be one tiniest portion of the Body of Christ. Ephesians 4:16 says that we are to be '. . . fitted and held together by that which every joint supplies, according to the proper working of each individual part . . .' As each transforming individual contributes that unique glory (1 Cor. 15:41–42) God created him to be, our joining supplies to each of us what we need from one another, as all are held together by love. That supply mutually equips, and the Body upbuilds. We need one another. No man is completely alone.

"Transformation is not the end product. It is the process by which we get there. Transformation proceeds within each individual by the presence and power of the Lord mainly through the company of Christ, but its purpose is not solely to present *individuals* without spot or wrinkle before the Father (Eph. 5:27), but a *Body* one in all its holy motives and desires. 'That he might present it to himself *a glorious church*, not having spot, or wrinkle, or any such thing; that it should be holy and without blemish.'"

The Enduement of Power

by Oswald J. Smith
Recommended by: Kenneth Steckel,
Pastor, Red Lion, Pennsylvania

The book by Oswald J. Smith, *The Enduement of Power*, has meant much to me as a pastor. This book and the revelation of God's Word unto me, has taught me the need to depend upon the Holy Spirit's power to be an effective pastor and preacher of God's Word. Romans 10:14 "How then shall they call on him whom they have not believed? and how shall they believe on him of whom they have not heard? and how shall they hear without a preacher?" Dr. Smith states God's plan is that everyone of us should live a spirit-filled life from the very moment of conversion if we are to be an effective vehicle of the Lord. The fact is, he says, practically no one does. Perhaps it is a lack of teaching. I do not know. According to Dr. Smith, the Bible distinguishes between "having the Holy Spirit, which is true of all believers, and being 'filled' with the Spirit, which is true of very few." The purpose of the Spirit's fullness is for the bestowal of power. "Tarry ye in the city until ye be endued with power from on high." St. Luke 24:49. The purpose of the Spirit's power is the bestowal of abilities to be witnesses. Acts 1:8 "But ye shall receive power, after that the Holy Ghost is come upon you: and ye shall be witnesses unto me both in Jerusalem, and in all Judea, and in Samaria, and unto the uttermost part of the earth."

"A merry heart doeth good like a medicine."
—Proverbs 17:22

The Problem of Pain

by C. S. Lewis
Recommended by: Rev. Ray Stedman,
Pastor, Author, Palo Alto, California

The one qualification which all human beings share without exception is that somewhere, and in some way, we all hurt. The hurt may be emotional or physical, but it can never be successfully avoided. Sometimes our hurts are fleeting and relatively light, and we can take them in stride, and other times they are so intense and powerful that we are tempted to despair and even suicide.

No book has helped me more to understand the reason for pain and its intended purpose in our lives than this sympathetic study by C. S. Lewis, first published in 1940. Perhaps no greater commentary on the purpose of pain has ever been made than this: "Pain insists upon being attended to. God whispers to us in our pleasures, speaks in our conscience, but shouts in our pains: it is His megaphone to rouse a deaf world." A page or two later he says, "No doubt, pain as God's megaphone is a terrible instrument; it may lead to final and unrepented rebellion. But it gives the only opportunity the bad man can have for amendment. It removes the veil; it plants the flag of truth within the fortress of a rebel soul."

Lewis probes the problem of pain much deeper than merely making an attempt to discover its purpose. He grounds the whole inquiry in a theological understanding of God and the universe. Nevertheless, the treatment is never merely pedantic. Even the average man or woman will find this book comes to grips with the distressing facts of life. In it, Lewis has given us his masterpiece.

Balancing the Christian Life

by Dr. Charles Ryrie
Recommended by: Paul E. Steele,
Pastor, Cupertino, California

I'm an enthusiast for Jesus Christ and like most enthusiasts tend to run hard after something I believe in. Also like most enthusiasts, I tend sometimes to focus too much on one aspect of a matter and not enough on the balancing truth. In other words, there is always a danger in my being out of balance.

For this reason, one of the books that has most influenced my life has been a book by Charles Ryrie, entitled *Balancing the Christian Life*. In a simple and concise manner, Dr. Ryrie deals with a number of practical areas where the Christian needs to maintain doctrinal equilibrium. His chapter of "Legalism" is worth the price of the book. He also carefully deals with the subjects of sanctification, dedication to God, money, and the love of God, the use of spiritual gifts and temptation. These and other helpful chapters should keep a believer from the spiritual vertigo that so often plagues us. It has been a blessing to me. I'm sure it will be to you as well.

"So some Christians are legalists, not because law is legalism, but because a wrong attitude, which any of us can have, is. Right living is letting the glory of God motivate every action and letting the Spirit of God empower them, including those things which we have to do in order to conform to the law of Christ."

Man's Search for Meaning

by Viktor Frankl
Recommended by: Paul W. Swets,
Pastor, Palm Springs, Florida

Nothing is as powerful as an idea whose time has come – especially when you are a young person starting out in life. – For me that powerful idea was found in *Man's Search for Meaning* by psychotherapist Viktor Frankl. First Frankl caught my attention by telling of his experience in a Nazi concentration camp during World War II. Then he built his philosophy (Logo therapy, he calls it) on the experience by asking: "What is the basic drive that keeps a person alive even in the most dire circumstances?"

Freud had claimed that man was dominated by the pleasure principle. Adler said it was a will-to-power. But in examining his own experience, Viktor Frankl found that the dominant principle was what he calls man's will-to-meaning; his deep-seated striving and struggling for a higher and ultimate meaning to his existence. He writes:

The first and foremost aim of mental hygiene should be to stimulate man's will-to-meaning . . . For to direct one's life toward a goal is of vital importance. There is nothing in the world, I dare say, which would so effectively help man to survive and keep healthy as would the knowledge of a life task. Thus we can understand the wisdom in the words of Nietzsche: "He who has a why to live for can bear almost any how. (p. 103)

I like that idea because it provides a powerful motive and adequate framework for setting one's life task in order. For me, ultimate meaning comes from a relationship to God. Built on that, life is wide open with meaning. The really important, primary question becomes not "What do I expect out of life?" but "What does the Author of life expect from me?"

Spiritual Leadership

by J. Oswald Sanders
Recommended by: Charles Swindoll,
Pastor, Fullerton, California

The nature of true spiritual leadership is indicated in a sentence from the pen of the late Dr. S. M. Zwemer: "There was never a world in greater need of men and women who know the way, and can keep ahead and draw others to follow." If we are to become leaders it will be because we can show the way to others, the way which we have successfully trodden ourselves. We can lead others only so far as we ourselves have gone, and we are leaders only to the extent that we inspire others to follow us. Because he himself has qualified, a leader can secure the co-operation of others in achieving some work for God.

In *Operation Victory*, Field Marshal Montgomery enunciates seven ingredients of military leadership which are equally applicable to the spiritual leader:

> He should be able to sit back and avoid getting immersed in detail.
> He must not be petty.
> He must not be pompous.
> He must be a good picker of men.
> He should trust those under him and let them get on with their job without interference.
> He must have the power of clear decision.
> He should inspire confidence.

Revival Lectures

by Charles G. Finney
Recommended by: R. Stanley Tam,
President, United States Plastic Corp.

Revival Lectures has inspired me to make my business a pulpit to present the gospel of Christ to our 53,000 customers across the United States. Year after year, 600 to 800 of our customers write to share how they have received Christ as their Saviour through the ministry of our business.

Charles G. Finney was the most widely known and successful American "revivalist" of his time. Trained for the teaching and legal professions when he was converted and called to preach, he became a minister to the masses, arguing at the bar of conscience concerning the eternal destiny of the human soul.

"A revival breaks the power of sin."

"Ordinarily, there are employed in the work of conversion three agents and one instrument. The agents are: God, some person who brings the truth to bear on the mind, and the sinner himself. The instrument is the truth."

"The ungodly are often led to conviction simply by the countenance of Christians."

. . . ye know that ye were not redeemed with corruptible things, as silver and gold, . . . but with the precious blood of Christ, as of a lamb without blemish and without spot.
—1 Peter 1:18,19

Hudson Taylor and a Booklet

Hudson sat in the warehouse and read a booklet. It was the reading of that little booklet that completely changed his outlook on life. Quite suddenly and unexpectedly it dawned upon him that what he had heard about God and Jesus Christ from his earliest childhood, was true. God was real. Jesus Christ was His son, and had died for the sake of sinners. He had come to life again, and was in heaven alive, able to see everything on earth – able to see him, right there in the warehouse! Everything was different now. The heavy feeling of discontent, the uneasy sensation of having done something wrong that would one day be found out, were gone. He felt free. It seemed too good to last!

(some years later in China)

Watchman Nee entered the room, sat down on one of the benches, and looked toward the little raised platform where Hudson Taylor was standing, reading aloud from the Bible. When Hudson closed his Bible and ceased preaching, Mr. Nee rose to his feet and said, "I have long sought the truth, as my father did before me, without finding it. I traveled far and near, searching for the way, but never found it. In the teachings of Confucius, the doctrines of Buddhism and Taoism, I have found no rest. But I have found rest in what we have heard tonight. Henceforth I am a believer in Jesus."

True Spirituality

by Dr. Francis Schaeffer
Recommended by: Cal Thomas,
Vice President, Moral Majority, Author, Speaker

In this book, I discovered the most profound thought I have yet encountered in the Christian life: that Christianity is true objectively. Regardless of the faith or lack of faith of men and women, God IS! Christ died and rose again and is coming again for His church! Man suffers from true moral guilt. My disbelief in the truth does not diminish truth any more than my sincere belief in falsehood makes a lie any less false or more true. In 1972, at the age of 30, this was an important breakthrough in my spiritual development.

True Spirituality also helped me understand the importance of a literally true, inspired and inerrant Bible; again, not because it HAS to be true or my faith is groundless, but because it IS true and attempts by theological liberals to reduce it are false.

The book also helped me to understand, for the first time, the reality of the spiritual or supernatural universe. Again, as Schaeffer puts it, the supernatural is objective reality. It doesn't exist because I say it does or want it to. It exists! It is a place, because the only One to come from there to here and return to there has told us so and has made reservations and guaranteed them for us in a dwelling place . . . a real place, not a philosophical place. Since reading *True Spirituality*, I have developed my own analogy. If we had the spiritual equivalent of longitude and latitude we could find Heaven, because it exists.

Schaeffer helped me in *True Spirituality*.

You're Someone Special

by Bruce Narramore
Recommended by: Lewis R. Timberlake,
CPAE, Professional Speaker

This book combines both theology and psychology to explain how God created us to be "winners." Dr. Narramore points out that we must choose less than God's best for our lives to be unsuccessful.

Even Christians feel that good self-esteem has no place in their lives when they've been taught to be humble, meek, and without pride. In *You're Someone Special*, Bruce Narramore reconciles that age-old conflict by using Scripture to prove that a good self-image is not only what God wants for His children, but also that a person can have good self-esteem and still be a humble Christian who is not full of sinful pride.

Dr. Narramore goes on to point out that the very fact that God created man in His own image elevates man above the animals (contrary to evolutionary teaching) and gives him great worth, significance and value. Man's knowledge and awareness of this worth is not humanistic self-centeredness, but simply esteem and respect for himself as God's creation.

You're Someone Special points out better than any other book I've ever read on self-esteem that a good self-image is not an attitude of prideful superiority, self-will, or self-centeredness. Rather, it is "valuing ourselves as equally important members of God's creation, seeing ourselves as (God's) image-bearers, (and) seeing ourselves as objects of divine love." Anyone who has ever had a problem in reconciling self-esteem and their Christian beliefs should read Dr. Narramore's book.

The Making of a Christian Leader

by Ted W. Engstrom
Recommended by: C. E. Toland,
President, Affiliated Food Stores, Inc.

I would like to recommend *The Making of a Christian Leader*, by Ted W. Engstrom. It has been my responsibility for several years to head up a management team consisting of ten to twenty people, and it has also been my privilege to attempt to teach young married couples in Sunday school. I believe that Ted Engstrom gives some of the most helpful information in explaining the role of leadership that I have ever heard or read. I highly recommend this book to any aspiring young leader:

"Outstanding results cannot be forced out of people. They occur only when individuals collaborate under a leader's stimulation and inspiration in striving toward a worthy common goal. Action is the key, because the leader and manager types are not mutually exclusive. The leader usually is a good manager, but a good manager is not necessarily a good leader because he may be weak in terms of motivating action in others.

"David illustrated clearly that the Christian leader, too, must be willing to exercise spiritual means to mold, stimulate and continually challenge his colleagues and subordinates.

"A leader has to recognize that he can only know himself as he is seen and experienced by others. He cannot be autonomous, but is an inseparable part of the group to which he belongs."

"A leader must be mindful that his emotional stability is indicated in the way he deals with people. Such characteristics as understanding, trust, confidence, tolerance, loyalty and sympathy are the ingredients that disclose emotional maturity."

Meditations and Devotions

by Elizabeth Fenn
Recommended by: Paul E. Toms,
Pastor, Boston

Francois de Fénelon, the seventeenth century devotional master, stimulates my thinking, and Elizabeth Fenn's book *Meditations and Devotions* is the best book I've found about him.

He served in the court of France's King Louis XIV, and the people of his day knew Fénelon as the "physician of souls." He wrote letters of encouragement to people, and that is mainly how he made his mark on the work of the Lord. He had a burning compassion for the lost and the suffering. Eventually he was banished from the king's court because of his commitment to the gospel.

As a pastor who counsels and encourages, I've found the letters of Fénelon instructive and inspirational. I recall, for instance, a letter he wrote to a woman who was having tremendous difficulty with her son. He was fatherly in explaining how to be patient with him, yet he was stern in urging her to remain firm in her stance for the Lord. This balance of understanding and firmness is something I've struggled with in my own ministry.

Fénelon's life reflected patience, and I have found this attribute especially inspirational. "We must stand still and adore Him (the Lord)" is one of the better-known quotes attributed to him.

*"And this is his commandment, that we should
. . . love one another."*
—I John 3:23

The Christian's Secret of a Happy Life
by Hannah Woodall Smith
Recommended by: Elmer L. Towns,
Dean, Liberty Baptist Seminary

A book that greatly influenced me is *The Christian's Secret of a Happy Life* by Hannah Woodall Smith. This book, first published in the late 1800s, has endured the test of time because it is well written and its message is easily understood. It has illustrations that the average Christian can relate to, and its principles are rooted in the Word of God.

When I first became a Christian at age 17, I was searching for stability and a deeper walk with Jesus Christ in my personal life. Obviously, I was reading the Scripture every day, and I began reading books to give me biblical principles by which I could govern my life. This book absorbed me in its reading so that I could not put it down. Like water on parched ground, it answered many questions I had regarding how to know Christ, how to get my prayers answered, how to have victory over sin, and how to relate to Jesus Christ through the Scripture.

This is one book that I have read several times; perhaps as many as two dozen readings. Each reading gives me a deeper understanding of the Lord Jesus Christ. When I was first saved, a friend told me, "Give priority to depth, and the breadth of ministry will take care of itself." I find that in *The Christian's Secret of a Happy Life* I have learned how to go deeper with God without being morbid. When the author offers a "happy life," I believe there is a reality in walking with Jesus Christ that the Christian can experience.

The Imitation of Christ

by Thomas à Kempis
Recommended by: Dr. Herb True, CPAE,
Certified Speaking Professional, Author

In prayer, God understands us . . . and we begin to understand God. Throughout the ages, in all countries and in all languages, there is not a book, excepting the Bible, which has inspired so many millions of readers in their prayer life as *The Imitation of Christ*. Since its first appearance in 1421 it has proven to be a timeless arsenal of moral armament and spiritual consolation. The style of the book is somewhat unusual, in which the reader finds Christ speaking to them in intimate conversation, seeking to make one fully aware of what it means to be a Christian. In these conversations, "Christ speaks" to the reader, drawing a picture of what transformation in Christ requires of the person and means for the society in which one lives. More than an outline of doctrine, each conversation brings its specific insight and suggestion. Those who are dedicated to the passion for speed and haste are told that, for them, patience must begin in tranquillity of action. For the inveterate inquirer into the will of God there is the gentle but firm message that to do God's will is to treat the circumstances of the moment for what they are – part of the Divine Plan for each of us. Those who cannot find the occasion to perform the works of mercy are made to see that every courtesy and kindness performed for the love of God is a work of mercy without price.

God Owns My Business

by Stanley Tam
Recommended by: Ron Useldinger, National Director,
Fitness Motivation Institute of America

The book that I feel has had the most influence on me in recent times is called *God Owns My Business,* by Stanley Tam. It is a book that helped me realize that without Jesus Christ in my life it would be impossible to understand what it means to work in faith. I believe the book has influened me in many ways, but mainly by giving me a reason to persist in working in faith. Money and material things are not the answer. If they stay with something long enough, everyone will suffer from burnout at sometime or other. With Christ owning my business, I believe that I can realize the true significance of why I am here on earth. If I honor Him, He will give me the fruit that I am seeking.

I have heard Mr. Tam speak in person and he has a great message for anyone, but even more so for the busy business person.

He came unto His own, and His own received Him not. But as many as received Him, to them gave He power to become the sons of God, even to them that believe on His name.
—John 1:11,12

Love Made Perfect

by Andrew Murray
Recommended by: Paul W. Valentine,
Pastor, Toledo, Ohio

"Of all gifts and experiences we have with and from the Lord – LOVE is still the greatest – what the World needs is LOVE – GOD is LOVE.

"Do you know the Love of God, and does it make you from morning to night sing the song of the ransomed ones? There is not a heart but says: 'Oh! I know the love of God too little.' And why is that? It is because you have not been perfected in love, because when the soul is perfected in love it has got such a sense of that love that it can rest in it for eternity, and though it has as much as it can contain for the time being it can always receive more. Again, is there no dissatisfaction with your love to God? You sometimes think that you can say 'Oh! my God, I do love Thee.' There are many Christians who don't say that – real Christians. They are afraid to say it. They fear God, and they say earnestly, 'I wish to love God,' and they complain very honestly and bitterly, 'Oh! my God. Why have I so little Love?'

"The child has not trouble in rejoicing in its parents' love. I remember my little boy or girl of five or six, sometimes coming to the study door and opening it, and just looking in and smiling to see papa's face; and then shutting the door and going away happy; or coming on tip-toe just outside the window, looking in to see papa, and then going off again to play.

"It was never an effort to the child to love the father. Dear Friends, God can do that for you, and make that His love shall all the day cover you, and that your love shall all the day rise up to Him in deep restfulness and in child-like peace. I am sure God can do it. I am sure God wants to do it, and this is what has brought us together. We need – more love, more of the love of God."

The Emotions of a Man

by Jerry Schmidt and Raymond Brock
Recommended by: Carl O. Vinger,
President, Vinger Marketing, Inc.

This book deals with emotions, and how they can be expressed by a man as a person, as a husband, as a father, and at his work. It also talks about the myth of being an old man; but, most importantly, it talks about being a whole man. The authors stress the importance of developing a lifestyle of balance.

In the final chapter, Schmidt and Brock say, "our model of manhood is Jesus Christ." "Who, being in very nature God, did not consider equality with God something to be grasped, but made himself nothing, taking the very nature of a servant, being made in the human likeness. And being found in appearance as a man, he humbled himself and became obedient to death – even death on a cross! Philippians 2:6–8 (NIV). The lifestyle of Christ is our goal. "Be imitators of God, therefore, as dearly loved children" Ephesians 5:1 (NIV)

Jesus was a man of faith, and of prayer. He was involved in the lives of people. He accepted them where they were, He gave people worth, and He required them to accept responsibility. Jesus also gave hope, encouragement and inspiration. He was a great teacher and helped reshape people's thinking, being assertive, straightforward and honest.

For ye are all the children of God by faith in Christ Jesus.

−Galatians 3:26

Where Is God When It Hurts

by Philip Yancey
Recommended by: Marvin Wall, Executive Director,
Canada, Christian Business Men's Committee Instructor

This book is a classic on the subject of pain. Many hard questions are asked and no easy, pat answers are given. The author has talked to Christians who suffer at a level far worse than most of us will ever experience. He has attempted, successfully I believe, to enter the world of the sufferer to find out what difference it makes to be a Christian there.

We could (some people do) believe that the purpose of life here is to be comfortable. Enjoy yourself, build a nice home, engorge good food, have sex, live the good life. That's all there is.

Yancey explains pain as God's megaphone which can drive me away from Him. I can hate God for allowing such misery or, on the other hand, it can drive me to Him. I can believe Him when He says this world is not all there is, and take the chance that He is making a perfect place for those who follow Him on pain racked earth. "He (God) has been there from the beginning designing a pain system that still, in the midst of a fallen, rebellious world, bears the stamp of His genius and equips us for life on the planet. He has allied Himself with the poor and suffering, establishing a kingdom tilted in their favour, which the rich and powerful often shun. He has joined us. He has hurt and bled and cried and suffered. He has dignified for all time those who suffer by sharing their pain."

This book has truly changed my view of pain and suffering and made me a more sensitive person to people's hurts and needs. I recommend it to all.

Birthright, Christian Do You Know Who You Are?

by David C. Needham
Recommended by: Joanne Wallace,
Author, President, Image Improvement, Inc.

This book outlines the answers to a healthy self-esteem and clarifies the secrets to the important question on one's identity. David Needham uses many anecdotes and illustrations to make his pages come alive with meaning. It encourages its readers to be motivated with who they are, and who HE is. I wish to use Mr. Needham's paragraph: "Contrary to much popular teaching, regeneration (being born again) is more than having something taken away (sins forgiven) or having something added to you (a new nature with the assistance of the Holy Spirit); it is becoming someone you had never been before. This new identity is not on the flesh level, but the spirit level – one's deepest self. This miracle is more than a "judicial" act of God. It is an act so REAL that it is right to say that a Christian's essential nature is righteous rather than sinful. All other lesser identities each of us has can only be understood and appreciated by our acceptance and response to this fact.

"But awareness of identity only brings us to the threshhold. Through the door now opened in front of us, the ultimate issue becomes not identity, but meaning or purpose in life based upon this awareness alone is the adequate foundation upon which one can confront sin and build a life of holiness."

"Trust in the Lord with all thine heart; and lean
not unto thine own understanding."
—Proverbs 3:5

The University of Hard Knocks

by Ralph Parlette
Recommended by: Dr. Tom Wallace,
Pastor, Louisville, Kentucky

Ralph Parlette's book, *The University of Hard Knocks*, was written the way he said it and not the way he would have written it. More than a million people heard the lectures, as given all over America. Parlette gave the series more than 2,500 times. Each lecture became a natural chapter for his book.

The author's use of the words, "bumps" and "knocks" instead of problems and trials, makes the reading fresh. Parlette deals with age-old principles and common, everyday experiences, but always dresses them in new suit language. On learning an obvious truth, he states, "I saw that for thirty years before I saw it."

The chapter on "Shake the Barrel" is a classic. A barrel of apples hauled over a bumpy road will soon have all the big apples on top and little ones settled to the bottom. He says that shaking and bumping reveals who will make it.

He deals with the "daily grind" with real insight. The quick flash and lightening approach to life is out, and the steady, day-by-day road will get one there, is his philosophy.

He says, "we can be pumpkins in one summer, with the accent on 'punk'. We can be mush melons in one day, with the accent on 'mush', but we cannot be oaks that way."

A chapter called "Go On South" deals with persistence in such a way that no one will ever be the same after exposing themselves to its three short pages. The ten chapters make excellent reading on a plane, in an airport, or in a hotel room.

Be the Leader You Were Meant To Be

by Leroy Eims
Recommended by: Draper Watson,
Funeral Director, President, Perry Chamber

Be the Leader You Were Meant To Be has become one of my favorite books. I turn to it very often because of what it says about Biblical principles of leadership. A person wanting to be a leader today must have inner strength and power, just as Moses, Gideon, Jeremiah, Paul, and Jesus did in their day. That power comes from God Himself. Scripturally, this book teaches how to live the life of a Christian leader and how to make an impact.

The inner life of a leader must be one of purity of life, humility, and child-like faith. A leader's attitude toward others must be one of JOY—Jesus first, others second, and yourself last. To lead is to serve, is a hard concept for many of us to grasp, but a leader must have a servant heart and a sensitive spirit.

Great leaders always strive for excellence, always have the initiative to make things happen, and are never afraid to be creative in trying new ideas. Great leaders make an impact by principles such as wholeheartedness, singlemindedness, and a fighting spirit. Wholeheartedness and zeal are outgrowths of a love that burns in a leader's heart. Singlemindedness is a characteristic that Paul had when he said, "I will press toward the mark." He didn't say he would glide or float toward the mark of the high calling of Christ Jesus. A leader will constantly face outer problems as well as inner problems and he must have a fighting spirit to combat them.

The entire book has many valuable lessons for life and each one of them is backed up by the Bible. I have read a lot of books on leadership but none that teaches Biblical principles in such a simple and straightforward way.

Pastors

The Christian Manifesto

by Francis Schaeffer
Recommended by: Bob Gehman,
Pastor, Reisterstown, Maryland

The Life of Adoniram Judson

Recommended by: Dr. Cecil Hodges,
Pastor, Savannah, Georgia

The Spiritual Man

by Watchman Nee
Recommended by: Charles Blair,
Pastor, Denver, Colorado

This book has ministered to my own heart as I have
studied and taught from it.

Holy Spirit, Who He Is
and What He Does

by R. A. Torrey
Recommended by: Bill Monroe
Pastor, Florence, S.C.

Pastors

The Denial of Death

by Ernest Becker
Recommended by: Richard Dowhower,
Senior Pastor, Camp Hill, Pennsylvania

My personal nomination of an outstanding book is Ernest Becker's Pulitzer Prize winner, *The Denial of Death*, first published in 1973 by The Free Press.

In addition to being a parish pastor seeking to comfort and encourage terminally ill parishioners, and later their grieving families, I experienced the book's impact on my life shortly after a decade in which I had buried my mother, my father, our infant son (from Sudden Infant Death Syndrome) and had to face at my fortieth birthday my own mortality in a new way.

In choosing Danish lay theologian, Soren Kierkegaard as having a better sense of the common denominator of human experience than Sigmund Freud, Becker, a California anthropology professor himself dying of cancer as he wrote it, gave me deeper insight into the human experience, a renewed confidence in God, and new courage to deal with death.

Such a gift frees us to live more fully and to Becker, I am grateful.

"For we know that if our earthly house of this
tabernacle were dissolved, we have a building
of God, an house not made with hands, eternal
in the heavens."

II Corinthians 5:1

Pastors

How to Live a Victorious Life

by Unknown Christian
Recommended by: Rev. Luke Weaver

I would like to recommend the book, *How to Live a Victorious Life*, signed by its author as the Unknown Christian. This book caused me to become established in the blessed assurance of salvation, and personal Christian victory many years ago, before I was in the ministry. I believe that it is the plan of God for every Christian to have the joy of the Lord every day of their life. The very foundation of joy is the Peace of God. As Jesus said in John 14:27, "Peace I leave with you, my peace I give unto you: not as the world giveth, give I unto you. Let not your heart be troubled, neither let it be afraid." Also, in John 15:11, "These things have I spoken unto you, that my joy might remain in you, and that your joy might be full."

Put God on Main Street

by Rex Humbard
Recommended by: Rev. John D. Castellani

In the summer of 1970, a member of my church gave me a book entitled. *Put God on Main Street*, written by Pastor Rex Humbard. While on vacation at Wildwood, New Jersey, I read this book through in which Rex explained the pain he endured and the faith he exercised in purchasing the property for the Cathedral for Tomorrow in Akron, Ohio.

This inspired me not to give up.

Down to Earth: Laws of Harvest

by John Lawrence
Recommended by: H. Skip Weitzen,
President, Foresight and Planning

This book is perhaps the most influential one I have read in the past decade. It makes me think each time I read it: Just as a farmer works with the laws of nature when sowing his seeds, my actions set into motion the laws of sowing which ultimately result in my own harvest. By understanding the few simple laws encompassing every human action and relationship, I came to realize that there is no escaping these laws, nor any exceptions to them.

Furthermore, the knowledge of sowing and reaping causes me to reappraise my values, motives and actions each day. I know that sowing "good" seeds today will produce a bountiful harvest in another season.

These laws are God's description of the way reality works. More importantly, I am learning that the laws of God (the Ten Commandments, the Beatitudes, and the Laws of the Harvest) are the most loving gift (next to His Son) that God could give to mankind.

Honour the Lord with thy substance, and with the first-fruits of all thine increase.
—Proverbs 3:9

12 Ways to Develop a Positive Attitude

by Dale Galloway
Recommended by: D. F. Whitaker,
Customer Service, USAir

This book provides the answers for ways to feel good about oneself and others. Here are some practical yet common quotations from Mr. Galloway which we have found helpful:

1) The prayer of serenity – "God grant me the serenity to accept the things I cannot change, courage to change the things I can and wisdom to know the difference."
2) "Let go and let God."
3) One especially helpful to young teenagers – "You are not inferior to anyone. Different, yes, wonderfully different but never inferior."
4) A great example of a positive Christian mind – "Whatever the mind can conceive and I will dare to believe, with God's help, I can achieve."

So many workable examples are given in this book, with many being quotations of others, such as The Prayer of Serenity. There is the example of Grandfather Limburger's mustache, telling us when we think the world stinks, we should take a look at ourselves; because, as Dr. Frankl discovered in his naked degradation, "no matter what happens each individual has the power to choose their own attitude and with the grace of God, and someone who cares enough to point the way, each individual can feel positive about themselves and others."

Behold the Lamb of God, which taketh away
the sin of the world.

—John 1:29

Confessions of a Happy Christian

by Zig Ziglar
Recommended by: Floyd Wickman,
Certified Speaking Professional

Hands down, the book that contributed the most in my life and seemed to be "talking" to me is Zig Ziglar's *Confessions of a Happy Christian*. Zig lets us know it's not only okay to become rich, it's our destiny if we choose it. His method of mixing the "spiritual" with the "practical" tells us you don't have to be a capitalistic "teetotaler" to believe in God nor a "tyrant" to become wealthy. There is a balance. When this balance is understood, things begin to happen in both areas.

"'For we walk by faith, not by sight.' And, 'Faith is a far better set of glasses than the believer has ever known before.' 'Twenty/twenty vision only satisfies until we know that there is something better.' That's what faith is. Something that's better than twenty/twenty vision—William Cook in Success Motivation and the Scriptures.*"*

THEOLOGICAL DEGREES
B.A.—Born Again
D.D.—Disturbing the Devil
Ph.D.—Past Having Doubt

Behold what manner of love the Father hath bestowed upon us that we should be called the sons of God.

—1 John 3:1

God's Miraculous Plan of Economy

by Jack Taylor
Recommended by: Rev. Jerry Williamson,
Pastor, Fort Lauderdale, Florida

Probably no other book in recent days has caught my attention and influenced my direction more than *God's Miraculous Plan of Economy*. From its outset, Mr. Taylor asks three questions: What is reality? Why are we here? What is God up to?

I especially like the statement, "The Christian lives in two realms or dimensions—the spiritual and the physical, or to put it another way, visible and invisible; or still another way, tangible and intangible. His ability to put those two realms in proper perspective with each other determines whether or not he succeeds as a Christian."

In addition to being a prolific writer, Jack Taylor is a good preacher. He uses a mix of his preaching and writing ability in this book. The following statement also caught my special attention: "Any plan of economy is constructed on a platform of principles. These may be right or wrong, but the plan will be as strong as the rightness or as weak as the wrongness of those principles." In the chapter, The Necessity of Neediness, we find, "That word N-E-E-D in Phillipians 4:19 is the hinge on which the whole verse swings. The more needs there are, the more God does, for God operates on the basis of need. If God is to do more, there must be more need. Need is the springboard of His doing! He only operates amid need."

There is much more in this book to challenge you to a life of faith in God. Get the book and get ready for a wealth of blessing.

Then said I, Here am I; send me.
—Isaiah 6:8

How to Make a Habit of Succeeding

by Mack R. Douglas
Recommended by: W. Heartsill Wilson, Sc. D, CPAE,
Certified Speaking Professional, Author

Many years ago a close and dear friend, Pat Zondervan, the Chairman of the Zondervan Publishing Company of Grand Rapids, sent me 'galley proofs' of an inspiring and thought-provoking book titled, *How to Make a Habit of Succeeding*, by Mack R. Douglas. I was impressed with the simplistic, yet dynamic, thoughts of the author.

SUCCESS is PURPOSE, GOALS and COMMITMENT united in a force-field of thrust equal to every challenge.

PURPOSE, Douglas believes, lies somewhere out in the future waiting to challenge, in an extraordinary way, the purpose of those who would claim the optimum is SUCCESS on an enduring and consistant basis. PURPOSE, indeed, is a long range power cell, lying in the future and awaiting the individual's quest for its ULTIMATE POWER.

Douglas states the PURPOSE may be intangible, but it is consistent and ever-present.

As for GOALS . . . they are much simpler in nature and easier to manage. GOALS should be made in increments that are clearly achievable, readily applied and finitely measurable. A tomorrow concept that when added to its gross capacity to engender SUCCESS—reaches far out into the tomorrows and finds its excellence in PURPOSE—sometimes reaching beyond purpose.

If, indeed, PURPOSE is preeminent and 'far-out' in SUCCESS planning and GOALS fill the space and void between the now and the PURPOSE—then the most imperative ingredient becomes COMMITMENT—the here-and-now element in SUCCESS.

"He careth for you."—I Peter 5:7

Balancing the Christian Life

by Charles Ryrie
Recommended by: Jack Wyrtzen,
Founder, Director, Word of Life Fellowship, Inc.

I read a book and I think of at least ten people whom I want to pass it on to. Sometimes it goes into the thousands! To recommend one book would be like me recommending my favorite book of the Bible, and that favorite book is the one I happen to be reading at the time. However, I think over the last ten years, the book that has meant more to me than any other is *Balancing the Christian Life*, by Charles Ryrie. It has some great chapters. For instance:

"How Are We Sanctified?"
"How Do We Use Our Money For The *Glory Of God?*"
"What About Our Spiritual Gifts?"
"How Can I Know If I'm Filled With The Spirit?"
"How Do I Face the Wiles Of The Devil?"
"Am I Legal Or Legalistic?"
"Should I Speak In Tongues?"
"Must Christ Be Lord To Be Savior?"

Ryrie says, "A spiritual Christian will exhibit at least two basic attitudes throughout life. The first is an attitude of thankfulness 'Giving thanks always for all things unto God and the Father in the name of our Lord Jesus Christ' (Eph. 5:20). . . . The other attitude of life which characterizes the spiritual Christian is, in the words of Paul, that of 'endeavoring to keep the unity of the Spirit in the bond of peace.' (Eph. 4:3)."

This book has helped more people to live a balanced Christian life than any other book I know of. We have all of our students at the Bible Institute read it.

P. J. Zondervan:
Books & Reading

Founder of Zondervan Publishing Company

Since I was a boy I have always had an appreciation for books and reading. The reading of books has made a tremendous impact on my life down through the years.

Of course the Bible is The Book, and my dad read it to us. This has always made an impact on me.

I often threatened to read *Pilgrim's Progress*, but I couldn't get into it. Then one day we began reading it at our family devotions. It made a tremendous impact on me – and on our family of children who were small at the time. They were as interested as I.

Reading the *Memoirs of Robert Murray McCheyne*, F. J. Huegel's *Bone of His Bone*, an Unknown Christian's *How To Live the Victorious Life* and *The Kneeling Christian*, R. A. Torrey's *The Power of Prayer and the Prayer of Power* have been a help in my life.

In books of daily devotions I've been greatly blessed by Oswald Chamber's *My Utmost for His Highest* and *Still Higher for His Highest*, by Andrew Murray's *God's Best Secrets*, by Eugenia Price's book *Share My Pleasant Stones*.

In inspirational books, I've been greatly blessed by reading V. Raymond Edman's book *They Found the Secret* and *The Saving Life of Christ* by E. M. Bounds.

GREAT THOUGHTS ON READING

Within that awful volume lies
The mystery of mysteries!
Happiest they of human race,
To whom God has granted grace
To read, to fear, to hope, to pray,
To lift the latch and force the way;
And better had they ne'er been born,
Who read to doubt, or read to scorn.

—Scott.

Church Libraries
Charles Haddon Spurgeon

A good library should be looked upon as an indispensable part of church furniture; and the deacons, whose business it is "to serve tables," will be wise if, without neglecting the table of the Lord, or of the poor, and without diminishing the supplies of the minister's dinner-table, they give an eye to his study-table, and keep it supplied with new works and standard books in fair abundance. It would be money well laid out, and would be productive far beyond expectation. Instead of waxing eloquent upon the declining power of the pulpit, leading men in the church should use the legitimate means for improving its power, by supplying the preacher with food for thought. Put the whip into the manger is my advice to all grumblers.

Some years ago I tried in induce our churches to have ministers' libraries as a matter of course, and some few thoughtful people saw the value of the suggestion, and commenced carrying it out. With much pleasure I have seen here and there the shelves provided, and a few volumes placed upon them. I earnestly wish that such a beginning had been made everywhere; but, alas! I fear that a long succession of starveling ministers will alone arouse the miserly to the conviction that parsimony with a minister is false economy. Those churches which cannot afford a liberal stipend should make some amends by founding a library as a permanent part of their establishment; and, by making additions to it from year to year, it would soon become very valuable. It may be objected that the books would be lost through change of users, but I would run the risk of that; and trustees, with a little care over the catalogue, could keep the libraries as securely as they keep the pews and pulpit.

G. Campbell Morgan on Reading

Campbell Morgan was yoked to a quick mind, and an insatiable desire for additional knowledge, which he acquired by reading, not only in youth but all through his life. A case in point is found in a letter in which he says: "At the age of twenty-five I was reading Wesley's *Journal*, and steeping myself in Kingsley, much to my advantage all my life."

A young minister once wrote him that he had difficulty in formulating his ideas and convictions into words. Dr. Morgan answered in a manner which showed his sympathy in the problem, and a desire to help in its solution. "Your difficulty is a real one. Of course, there are those who have a natural gift in this direction. Where this is lacking, a great deal may be done by reading some of the best masters, noticing carefully their method in the use of words and the formation of sentences. What is pre-eminently necessary is an enlarged vocabulary, and this such reading will help to supply. Let every new word be noted, and its true value learned. Where this is done with patience, it will be found in course of time that such words come naturally into use." The method was one which he himself had found helpful.

The Saviour who fitted before the patriarchs through the fog of the old dispensation, and who spake in time past to the fathers by the prophets, articulate but unseen, is the same Saviour who, on the open heights of the Gospel, and in the abundant daylight of this New Testament, speaks to us. Still all along it is the same Jesus, and that Bible is from beginning to end, all of it, the word of Christ.

—James Hamilton

Oswald Chambers on Study

Study to begin with can never be easy; the determination to form systematic mental habits is the only secret. Don't begin anything with reluctance.

Inspiration won't come irrespective of study, but only because of it. Don't trust to inspiration, use your own 'axe'. (Psalm lxxiv. 5) Work! Think! Don't luxuriate on the mount!

Note two things about your intelligence: first, when your intelligence feels numb, quit at once, and play or sleep; for the time being the brain must recuperate; second, when you feel a fidget of associated ideas, take yourself sternly in hand and say, 'You shall study, so it's no use whining.'

In beginning to study a new subject you do it by repeated starts until you get your mind into a certain channel, after that the subject becomes full of sustained interest.

It is better for your mental life to study several subjects at once rather than one alone. What exhausts the brain is not *using* it, but abusing it by nervous waste in other directions. As a general rule, the brain can never do too much.

Irritation may be simply the result of not using your brain. Remember, the brain gets exhausted when it is not doing anything.

Fulton Sheen on Study

My reading embraces literature, science, philosophy of politics—in a word everything that would be useful for a priest in instructing or discoursing with others, or in supplying material for communication. I never read novels. When I was in college, I had great difficulty reading all of the novels assigned in class, but I do read book reviews of novels and also studies of contemporary literature which summarize their trends.

The first subject of all to be studied is Scripture, and this demands not only the reading of it, but the study of commentaries. For practical purposes and for the busy priest, I have found no commentary to equal the *Daily Study Bible* of William Barclay, which appeared in about fifteen small volumes. Protestant commentaries, I discovered, were also particularly interesting because Protestants have spent more time on Scripture than most of us. In general, I found Arthur W. Pink's three-volume *Exposition of the Gospel of St. John* to be one of the best from a spiritual point of view.

. . . these are written that ye might believe that Jesus is the Christ, the Son of God and that believing ye might have life through his name.
—John 20:31

Emmet Fox on Study

For the spiritual study of the Bible, by far the best edition to use is the ordinary King James version. Have a Bible with type large enough to be read with comfort. A dollar or two extra spent on your Bible is worth while since you do not buy one every day.

As a general rule, it is not well to work through the Bible steadily from end to end, but rather to select any portion as you feel led at the time. Whichever section interests you most at the moment is usually likely to be best for you at the time. Read the Bible in the light of the spiritual interpretation, using the principal keys and symbols, noting the meanings of proper names, and so forth, as you come to them.

The Bible will usually give you a special message for yourself, fitting your need at the moment. In order to get this, you should claim frequently while you are reading: *"Divine Intelligence is inspiring me."*

Do not go to the Bible to get confirmation for your own ideas, but rather to be taught something new.

"Speak Lord, for Thy servant heareth."

These things have I written unto you that believe on the name of the Son of God; that ye may know that ye have eternal life, and that ye may believe on the name of the Son of God.

—1 John 5:13

John R. W. Stott on Study

There is a freshness and a vitality about every sermon which is born of study; without study, however, our eyes become glazed, our breath stale and our touch clumsy. 'The preacher's life must be a life of large accumulation,' said Bishop Phillips Brooks in his 1877 Yale Lectures. He went on:

He must not be always trying to make sermons, but always seeking truth, and out of the truth which he has won the sermons will make themselves . . . Here is the need of broad and generous culture. Learn to study for the sake of truth, learn to think for the profit and the joy of thinking. Then your sermons shall be like the leaping of a fountain, and not like the pumping of a pump.

The best-known living evangelist addresses the same exhortation to preachers today. Speaking to about 600 clergy in London in November 1979, Billy Graham said that, if he had his ministry all over again, he would make two changes. People looked startled. What could he possibly mean? First, he continued, he would study three times as much as he had done. He would take on fewer engagements. 'I've preached too much,' he said, 'and studied too little.' The second change was that he would give more time to prayer. Moreover, in making these emphases, he must have been deliberately echoing the apostolic resolve: 'we will devote ourselves to prayer and to the ministry of the Word.' (Acts 6:4) Because afterwards I commented appreciatively on what he had said, Dr. Graham wrote to me the following day and added: 'I remember that Dr. Donald Grey Barnhouse once said: "If I had only three years to serve the Lord, I would spend two of them studying and preparing."'

Educators

Dr. Robert Milligan

former President, College of the Bible, Univ. of Kentucky

It is very well to understand the book of nature, and to be well read in the whole encyclopedia of the sciences, literature, and the arts; but, at the same time, it is well to remember that there is nothing in all of these that can either justify, or sanctify or redeem a soul. A man might preach eloquently on natural science, and metaphysics, and politics all his life, and lie down in sorrow at last, to suffer as keenly from the piercings of the undying worm, and from the flames of the unquenchable fire as the most ignorant and stupid of his admiring auditors.

Dr. Raymond Muncy

Professor of History, Harding University

The word of God repeatedly encourages us to use our minds, to think, to meditate, and to contemplate. The very first Psalm says, "Happy is the man who does not walk in the path of the ungodly, or who does not stand in the way of sinners, or who does not sit in the seat of the scornful. For his delight is in the law of the Lord and in his law doth he meditate day and night." The apostle Paul wrote to the brethren at Philippi, "Finally, brothers, whatever is lovely, what ever is admirable – if anything is excellent or praiseworthy – think about such things." It seems to me that the apostle to the Gentiles has summed up the entire educational process.

There is no better definition of Christian education than this, and we are encouraged to THINK, to THINK about THINKING.

BIBLIOGRAPHY
of Recommended Books Currently in Print

a Kempis, Thomas. *The Imitation of Christ*. Moody Press, 1980.

Acklund, Donald F. *Moving Heaven and Earth*.

Adams, Lane. *How Come It's Taking Me So Long to Get Better?* Tyndale House, 1977.

Allen, Charles. *Life More Abundant*. Jove, 1976.

Allen, James. *As a Man Thinketh*. Executive Books, 1984.

Armerding, Hudson. *Leadership*. Tyndale House, 1978.

Arp, Dave & Claudia. *Ten Dates for Mates*. Thomas Nelson, 1983.

Augsburger, David. *When Caring Is Not Enough*. Herald Press, 1983.

Augustine. *City of God*. Doubleday.

Bancroft, Emery. *Elemental Theology*. Zondervan, 1977.

Barnhouse, Donald, *Romans*. Randall House, 1975.

Becker, Ernest. *The Denial of Death*. Free Press, 1973.

Bell, Grover. *Here's How by Who's Who*. Distributed by Executive Books.

Blanchard, Kenneth, & Johnson, Spencer. *The One Minute Manager*. Berkley, 1983.

Bounds, E. M. *Power Through Prayer*. Whitaker House, 1983.

Bowman, George. *How To Succeed With Your Money*. Moody.

Brainerd, David. *Life of David Brainerd*. Baker Book House, 1978.

Bridges, Jerry. *The Pursuit of Holiness*. Navpress, 1978.

Brother Andrew. *God's Smuggler*. NAL, 1968.

Brown, Stephen. *If God is in Charge*. Thomas Nelson Pub.

Bruce, A. B. *The Training of the Twelve*. Keats Pub.

Buchan, John. *Thirty Nine Steps*. Biblio Distribution, 1975.

Bunyan, John. *Pilgrim's Progress*. NAL.

Butterfield, Herbert. *Christianity and History*. Oxford Univ., 1979.

Chafer, Lewis. *Grace*. Zondervan.

Chafer, Lewis. *He That Is Spiritual*. Zondervan, 1918.

Chambers, Oswald. *God's Workmanship*. Christian Literature Crusade.

———. *My Utmost for His Highest*. Dodd, Mead.

———. *Still Higher for His Highest*. Christian Literature Crusade, 1970.

Chesterton, G. K. *The Everlasting Man*. Doubleday, 1974.

Cho, Paul. *The Fourth Dimension*. Bridge, 1979.

Churchill, Winston. *A History of the English Speaking Peoples*. Dodd, Mead & Co., 1957.

Clason, George. *The Richest Man in Babylon*. Hawthorn, 1955.

Coleman, Robert, *Master Plan of Evangelism*. Revell 1963.

Colson, Charles. *Born Again*. Bantam, 1976.

———. *Loving God*. Zondervan, 1983.

Cook, William. *Success, Motivation, and the Scriptures*. Broadman, 1975.

Costantino, Frank. *Holes in Time*. Acclaimed Books.

Danforth, William H. *I Dare You*. I Dare You Publishers.

Day, Richard. *Bush Aglow*. Judson Press, 1936.

Dayton, Edward, & Engstrom, Ted. *Strategy for Living*. Regal, 1976.

Douglas, Mack. *How To Make a Habit of Succeeding*. Zondervan.

Drummond, Henry. *The Greatest Thing in the World*. Whitaker House, 1981.

Edgar, Thomas. *Miraculous Gifts*. Loizeaux, 1983.

Edwards, Jonathan. *The Sermons of Jonathan Edwards*. Greenwood.

Eims, Leroy. *Be the Leader You Were Meant to Be*. Victor Books, 1975.

Ellul, Jacques. *The Presence of the Kingdom*. Seabury, 1967. *Ethics of Freedom*.

Engstrom, Ted. *The Making of a Christian Leader*. Zondervan, 1976.

Erwin, Gayle. *The Jesus Style*. Ronald Haynes Pub., 1983.

Faut & Pinson. *Twenty Centuries of Great Preaching*.

Fenn, Elizabeth. *Meditations and Devotions*.

Finney, Charles. *Revival Lectures*. Fleming Revell.

Foster, Richard. *Freedom of Simplicity*. Harper & Row, 1981.

Fox, Emmet, *The Sermon on the Mount*. Harper & Row, 1934.

Frankl, Viktor. *Man's Search for Meaning*. Pocket Books, 1980.

Friesen, Garry. *Decision Making and the Will of God*. Multnomah, 1983.

Galloway, Dale. *12 Ways to Develop a Positive Attitude*. Tyndale House, 1975.

Gordon, Ernest. *Through the Valley of the Kwai*. Harper & Bros., 1962.

Gordon, Samuel. *Quiet Talks on Power*. Putnam Pub Group, 1960.

Graham, Billy. *Peace With God*. Doubleday, 1953.

Grant, Dave. *The Ultimate Power*. Fleming Revell, 1983.

Gregory, John. *The Seven Laws of Teaching*. PBBC Press, 1976.

Grubb, Norman. *The Law of Faith*. Christian Literature Crusade, 1969.

————. *The Life of Missionary C. T. Studd*. Christian Literature, 1972.

————. *Rees Howells, Intercessor*. Christian Literature, 1967.

Haggai, John. *How to Win Over Worry*, Zondervan, 1959.

Hagin, Ken. *The Authority of the Believer*.

Hendricks, Olan. *Management for the Christian Leader*. Zondervan.

Hall, Douglas. *Not Made for Defeat*. Attic Press, 1970.

Hallesley, O. *Temperament and the Christian Faith*.

Herbert, Frank, and Ransom, Bill. *The Lazarus Effect*. Putnam Pub Group, 1983.

Herrod, Ron. *Faith Under Fire*. Daniels Publishing.

Heywood, Robert. *The Works of the Mind*. University of Chicago.

Hill, Gene. *A Hunter's Fireside Book*. Winchester Press, 1.

Hubbard, David. *The Holy Spirit in Today's World*.

Humbard, Rex. *Put God on Main Street*.

Hurnard, Hannah. *Hind's Feet on High Places*. Tyndale Pub.

Huss, John. *Robert G. Lee, The Authorized Biography*. Zondervan, 1967.

Institute in Basic Youth Conflicts. *Character Sketches from the Pages of Scripture*. Inst. in Basic Youth Conflicts.

Joergenson, Johannes. *St. Francis of Assisi*.

Jones, Bob Sr. *Things I Have Learned*. Bob Jones Univ.

Jones, Charles. *Life Is Tremendous*. Tyndale House.

Jones, E. Stanley. *Abundant Living*. Abington, 1976.

————. *Christ at The Round Table*. Century Book Bindery, 1928.

Jones, Martin Lloyd. *Preaching and Preachers*.

Kane, J. Herbert. *Understanding Christian Missions*. Baker Book House.

Kramer, Jerry. *Instant Replay*. NAL, 1969.

LaHaye, Tim. *Spirit-Controlled Temperament*. Tyndale.

Laidlaw, Robert. *The Reason Why*. Zondervan, 1975.

Lambert, D. W. *Oswald Chambers: An Unbribed Soul*. Christian Literature Crusade, 1968.

Law, William. *A Serious Call to Holy Life*. Biblio, 1976.

Lawrence, John. *Down to Earth: Laws of Harvest*. Tyndale.

Lawson, James. *Deeper Experiences of Famous Christians*. Warner Press, 1981.

Leopold, Aldo. *Sand County Almanac*. Tamarack Press, 1977.

Lewis, C. S. *God in the Dock*. Wm. B. Eerdmans, 1970.

Lewis, C. S. *Mere Christianity*. Macmillan, 1964.

Lewis, C. S. *Perelandra*, Macmillan, 1968.

Lewis, C. S. *The Problem of Pain*. Macmillan, 1978.

Lewis, C. S. *The Weight of Glory and Other Addresses.* Macmillan, 1980.

Lewis, C. S. *Your God Is Too Small.* Macmillan.

Lindsell, Harold, *The Battle for the Bible.* Zondervan, 1978.

Lindsey, Hal. *1980 Countdown to Armageddon.* Bantam.

Lloyd-Jones, D. Martyn. *Study of Romans.* Zondervan.

Loane, Marcus. *Makers of Religious Freedom.* Eerdmans.

Lutzer, Erwin. *Failure: The Back Door to Success.* Moody.

Luther, Martin. *Large Catechism.*

MacAuthor, John. *Found: God's Will.* Victor Books, 1977.

Mandino, Og. *Greatest Success in the World.* Bantam, 1982.

Mantle, J. Gregory. *Beyond Humiliation, The Way of the Cross.* Bethany House, 1975.

Marshall, Peter, and Manuel, David. *The Light and the Glory.* Fleming Revell, 1981.

May, William. *A Catalogue of Sins.* Holt, Rinehart & Winston, 1967.

McConkey, Wm. *Threefold Secret of the Holy Spirit.* Back To The Bible.

McDowell, Josh and Stewart, Don. *Answers to Tough Questions.* Campus Crusade, 1980.

Meilaender, Gilbert. *The Taste for the Other.* Wm. B. Eerdmans Publishing.

Merrill, Dean. *Another Chance . . . How God Overrides Our Big Mistakes.* Zondervan, 1981.

Meyer, F. B. *Shepherd Psalm.* Moody Press, 1976.

Miller, Basil. *George Mueller, Man of Faith & Miracles.* Bethany House, 1972.

Morgan, G. Campbell. *The Crises of the Christ.* Fleming Revell, 1954.

Morgan, G. Campbell. *Living Messages of the Books of the Bible.*

Morgan, Jill. *A Man of the Word.* Baker Books, 1960.

Mueller, George. *A Life of Trust.*

Morris, Henry. *That You Might Believe.* Good News.

Murray, Andrew. *Love Made Perfect.*

Murray, Andrew. *God's Best Secrets*. Zondervan, 1957.

Murray, Andrew. *With Christ in the School of Prayer*. Whitaker House, 1981.

Narramore, Bruce. *You're Someone Special*. Zondervan, 1980.

Nee, Watchman. *The Normal Christian Life*. Tyndale, 1977.

Nee, Watchman. *The Spiritual Man*. Christian Fellowship, 1968.

Needham, David. *Birthright, Christian Do You Know Who You Are*. Multnomah, 1981.

Newell, William. *Romans Verse by Verse*. Moody Press, 1938.

Olt, Russell. *Prophet to India*. Warner Press, 1930.

Olson, Bruce. *Bruchko*. Creation House.

Packer, J. I. *Evangelism and the Sovereignty of God*. Inter-Varsity Press, 1961.

Packer, J. I. *Knowing God*. InterVarsity Press, 1973.

Palmer, Sara C. *The Bishop of Wall Street*.

Parlette, Ralph. *The University of Hard Knocks*. Brownlow, 1966.

Pascal, Blaise. *Pensees*. Biblio Distribution, 1973.

Penney, J. C. *Christian Principles in Business*.

Phillips, J. B. *Your God Is Too Small*, MacMillan.

Pink, Arthur. *The Sovereignty of God*. Baker Books, 1977.

Polston, Don. *Living Without Losing*. Harvest House, 1975.

Prest, John. *Garden of Eden*. Yale University Press.

Rainsford, Marcus. *Our Lord Prays for His Own*.

Rayburn, Jim III. *Dance, People, Dance*. Tyndale House.

Redpath, Alan. *The Making of a Man of God*. Fleming Revell, 1962.

Redpath, Alan. *Victorious Christian Living*. Fleming Revell, 1955.

Richardson, Don. *The Lords of the Earth*. Regal, 1977.

Robertson, Pat. *The Secret Kingdom*. Thomas Nelson, 1982.

Rolls, Charles. *The Indescribable Christ*. Loizeaux, 1983.

Ryrie, Charles. *Balancing the Christian Life*. Moody Press, 1969.

Sanders, J. Oswald. *A Spiritual Clinic*. Moody Press, 1958.

Sanders, J. Oswald. *Spiritual Leadership*. Moody Press, 1974.

Sandford, John and Paula. *The Transformation of the Inner Man*. Bridge Publishing, Inc., 1982.

Schaeffer, Francis. *A Christian Manifesto*. Good News, 1981.

Schaeffer, Francis. *The Great Evangelical Disaster*. Good News, 1984.

Schaeffer, Francis. *How Should We Then Live?* Good News, 1983.

Schaeffer, Francis. *The Mark of a Christian*. InterVarsity Press, 1970.

Schaeffer, Francis. *True Spirituality*. Tyndale House.

Schmidt, Jerry and Brock, Raymond. *The Emotions of a Man*. Harvest House, 1983.

Schuller, Robert. *Tough Times Never Last, But Tough People Do*. Thomas Nelson, 1983.

Schuller, Robert. *Move Ahead With Possibility Thinking*.

Shelley, Mary. *Frankenstein*. NAL.

Shephard, Esther. *Paul Bunyan*. Harcourt, Brace, Jovanovich, 1941.

Shoemaker, Sam. *Extraordinary Living for Ordinary Man*. Zondervan, 1965.

Simpson, A. B. *The Christ Life*. Christian Publications.

Smalley, Gary. *If Only He Knew*. Zondervan, 1982.

Smalley, Gary. *For Better or for Best*. Zondervan.

Smith, Hannah. *The Christian's Secret of a Happy Life*. Whitaker House, 1983.

Smith, Malcolm. *How I Learned to Meditate*.

Smith, Oswald J. *The Enduement of Power*.

Smith, Wilbur. *Treasury of Books*. Baker Pub.

Spring, Gardiner. *Distinguishing Traits of a Christian*. Presby and Reformed, 1966.

Spurgeon, Charles. *Lectures to My Students*. Zondervan, 1980.

———. *Morning and Evening*. Baker Book House, 1975.

———. *Spurgeon's Devotional Bible*. Baker Book House, 1974.

———. *Shadow of the Broadbrim*

Stanford, Miles. *The Green Letters: Principals of Spiritual Growth*. Zondervan, 1975.

Stedman, Ray. *Authentic Christianity*. Word Pub.

Stevenson, Robert Louis. *Treasure Island*. Penguin, 1975.

Stone, Irving. *The Agony and the Ecstasy*. Doubleday.

Stormer, John H. *None Dare Call It Treason*.

Strong, James. *Strong's Concordance*. Thomas Nelson, 1980.

Swindoll, Charles. *Growing Strong in the Seasons of Life*. Multnomah, 1983.

———. *Strengthening Your Grip*. Word, 1982.

———. *Three Steps Forward, Two Steps Backward*. Thomas Nelson, 1980.

———. *Encourage Me*. Multnomah, 1982.

Tam, Stanley. *God Owns My Business*. Horizon House, 1984.

Taylor, Howard and Mary. *Hudson Taylor's Spiritual Secret*. Moody Press.

Taylor, Jack. *God's Miraculous Plan of Economy*. Broadman, 1975.

Thomas, Henry and Dana. *Living Biographies of Religious Leaders*. Perma Giants. 1942.

Thomas, W. Ian. *The Mystery of Godliness*. Zondervan, 1964.

———. *The Saving Life of Christ*. Zondervan, 1961.

Tolkien, J. R. *The Lord of the Rings*. Houghton Mifflin, 1974.

Torrey, R. A. *How to Pray*. Moody Press.

———. *Treasury of Scripture Knowledge*. Fleming Revell, 1973.

———. *Holy Spirit, Who He Is and What He Does*. Revell, 1927.

————. *What the Bible Teaches.* Fleming Revell.

Tournier, Paul. *Adventure of Living.* Harper & Row, 1976.

Tozer, A. W. *The Knowledge of the Holy.* Harper & Row, 1978.

————. *The Pursuit of God.* Fleming Revell, 1982.

————. *That Incredible Christian.* Christian Publications, 1964.

Tsai, Christiana. *Jewels from the Queen of the Dark Chamber.* Moody Press, 1982.

Trumbull, Charles. *The Life that Wins.*

Unamuno, Miguel. *The Tragic Sense of Life.* Dover Publications.

Wagner, Maurice. *The Sensation of Being Somebody.* Zondervan, 1975.

Wead, Doug. *The Compassionate Touch.* Bethany House, 1980.

White, John. *Fight, Practical Handbook for Christian Living.* Inter-Varsity, 1976.

Wilkerson, Dave. *The Cross and the Switchblade.* Jove, 1983.

Woodruff, James. *The Aroma of Christ.* G. T. Press, 1981.

Wright, H. Norman. *Communications: Key to Your Marriage.* Regal. 1979.

Yancey, Philip. *Where Is God When It Hurts.* Zondervan.

Ziglar, Zig. *Confessions of a Happy Christian.* Pelican, 1982.

For additional reading lists or children's reading contracts send stamped self addressed envelope to:

Life Management Services, Inc.
Box 1044
Harrisburg, PA 17108
717-763-1950